Praise for BREAKING RANKS

"Military service is an integral part of life in Israel: both men and women serve in the Israel Defense Forces; devotion to the country's survival is a given. So disobeying an order is a remarkable action—one discussed in depth here by nine 'refuseniks,' Israeli soldiers who refused to serve in the Occupied Territories. They tell Chacham...about their upbringings, their crises of conscience, the mistreatment of Palestinians by themselves and others, their attempt to reconcile support for Palestinian rights with devotion to their homeland, their refusals to serve, and the consequences. Anyone trying to understand why these men have taken the action they have will be moved by their thoughtfulness and articulateness."

—Publishers Weekly

"In *Breaking Ranks*, we hear the voices of men who have refused to participate in the atrocity-producing situation of military occupiers. We learn of their admirable personal struggles in overcoming psychic numbing and recognizing the pain and humiliation they and others were inflicting. Their actions have extraordinary significance for the State of Israel, for the Palestinians, and for the rest of us as well."

—Robert Jay Lifton, author of *Destroying the World to Save It:
Aum Shinrikyo, Apocalyptic Violence, and the New Global Terrorism*

"This book should be read by those of all political views concerning the Israeli-Palestinian conflict. These accounts and interviews will surprise, sadden, shock, infuriate, but most of all, stimulate open-minded readers to consider alternatives to their strongly held views. This is an ultimately hopeful book. I was profoundly moved by it."

—David Gordis, President, Hebrew College

"Ronit Chacham's exemplary oral history and commentaries ... ray in depressing yet hopeful detail those coura... who have refused to participate as soldie... ls.... An end to the bitter civil war may ... hese remarkable men to prove that war ... that some are brave enough to say 'No.'"

—The Jewish Peace Fellowship

Breaking Ranks

REFUSING TO SERVE IN THE
WEST BANK AND GAZA STRIP

RONIT CHACHAM

Other Press • New York

Production Editor: Robert D. Hack

This book was set in Fournier and DIN by Tina Thompson.
Design by Miko McGinty. Maps by Rita Jules.

First softcover printing 2003. ISBN 1-59051-099-2

10 9 8 7 6 5 4 3 2 1

Library of Congress Cataloging-in-Publication Data

Chacham, Ronit.
    Breaking ranks : refusing to serve in the West Bank and Gaza Strip / Ronit
Chacham.
        p. cm.
    Includes maps.
    ISBN 1-59051-043-7
    1. Conscientious objectors—Israel. 2. Israel. Tseva haganah le-Yisrael—
Reserves. 3. Arab-Israeli conflict—1993—Moral and ethical aspects—Israel.
I. Title.

    UB345.I75 C53 2003
    355.2'24'095694—dc21

                                                2002035486

CONTENTS

ACKNOWLEDGMENTS

Many people were involved in the making of this book, and I feel incredibly fortunate to have received so much help that was endowed with such kindness.

I wish to thank Rachel Jones, from New York, who worked with great dedication on the first draft of the translation of the interviews. I am much obliged to Blake Radcliffe from Other Press, who very patiently bore with me and very skillfully edited the text in English. Special thanks to Susan Fairfield from Other Press, who edited the introduction and followed the book through many of its stages with great care.

I wish to thank Victor Gurewich in Boston, whose idea it was that such a book should be published in the U.S. to inform the American public about the testimonies of combat soldiers who had publicly denounced the occupation and its effect on the future of Israel. I also owe gratitude to Simone Bitton in Paris, who suggested that I write the book. Once I had decided to take up this task, I contacted Ishai Menuchin, founder of Yesh Gvul, the first refusenik movement in Israel. He is one of the people who has kept the flame of civil disobedience alive for twenty years, even in times when nobody wanted to listen. He was a great help and gave me guidance and all the contacts I needed to get started on this venture.

I thank my friends in Israel who read the manuscript, made suggestions, and offered advice: Tikva Honing Paranss, who gave me pointed criticism; Iris Mizrahi, Yael Lerer, Michal Chacham-Dallal, and Osnat Trabelsi, who made helpful suggestions; Adi Offir of Tel Aviv University, a veteran refusenik who continues to be a source of inspiration and strength to his refusenik students and asked me guiding questions; Hulda Raz, who checked all the biblical references; and Anahit Herson, who worked on the transcription of the interviews.

Thanks also to Michel Feher and Amanda Bay of Paris, who read the manuscript many times over and offered their insights; Freddy Dreseen of Belle Île; Amit Mashiach, the Courage to Refuse spokesman; Sergeiy Sandler of New Profile; Judith Feher Gurewich, my tireless and extremely dedicated editor, who spent hours on end reading and restructuring the work and helped with the endless versions of the introduction; and Amnon Raz Krakotzkin, who has always been my perceptive and knowledgeable guiding adviser.

And, of course, I want to thank the refuseniks I met, who were all extremely cooperative, among them Idan Landau, Mike Levine, Noam Kozar, and especially Assaf Oron, Rami Kaplan, Yaniv Iczkovitz, Shamai Leibowitz, Guy Grossman, Yuval Lotem, Ishay Rosen-Zvi, Tal Belo, and David Chacham-Herson. I remain dearly indebted to you all. May you have the courage to ask more questions and offer visions that will redeem this wounded country.

Jerusalem, August 2002

INTRODUCTION

Landmarks in the Israeli– Palestinian Conflict

On January 25, 2002, a quarter-page letter appeared in the Israeli daily newspaper *Ha'aretz*. Fifty-two soldiers and officers of the Israeli army reserves, including captains, called on their comrades-in-arms to join their act of refusal to serve in the occupied Palestinian territories of the West Bank and the Gaza Strip.[1] This refusal followed the reservists' realization that, instead of bringing an end to the occupation, the 1993 Oslo Accords between Israel and the Palestinians were being violated by Israel. Israel had withdrawn only partially from the occupied territories, and, while the settlements in the West Bank and Gaza Strip were supposed to be dismantled, they were in fact being expanded. The reservists were particularly disturbed by the force they were expected to use as soldiers against a civilian population collectively penalized for its uprising against the occupation, long before Palestinian suicide bombers started to explode in Israeli streets.

This is the text of their letter:

DECLARATION OF ISRAELI COMBATANT RESERVISTS:
A REFUSAL TO SERVE IN THE WEST BANK AND GAZA STRIP

We, reserve combat officers and soldiers of the Israeli Defense Forces, who were raised in the principles of Zionism, sacrifice, and giving to

---

1. Eight months after the publication of the letter, 480 soldiers and officers had added their names to the list.

the people of Israel and to the State of Israel, who have always served in the front lines, and who were the first to carry out any mission, light or heavy, in order to protect the State of Israel and strengthen it;

We, combat officers and soldiers who have served the State of Israel for long weeks every year, in spite of the dear cost to our personal lives, have been on reserve duty throughout the occupied territories and were issued commands and directives that had nothing to do with the security of our country, and that had the sole purpose of perpetuating our control over the Palestinian people;

We, whose eyes have seen the bloody toll this exacts from both sides;

We, who believed that the commands issued to us in the territories destroy all the values we had absorbed while growing up in this country;

We, who understand now that the price of occupation is the loss of the IDF's[2] human character and the corruption of the entire Israeli society;

We, who know that the territories are not Israel, and that all settlements are bound to be evacuated in the end:

We hereby declare that we shall not continue to fight this war of the settlements.

We shall not continue to fight beyond the 1967 borders in order to dominate, expel, starve, and humiliate an entire people.

We hereby declare that we shall continue serving in the Israeli Defense Forces in any mission that serves Israel's defense.

The missions of occupation and oppression do not serve this purpose, and we shall take no part in them.

---

2. Israeli Defense Forces.

The new movement was called Ometz leSarev: Courage to Refuse. For the refuseniks, as they came to be called, denouncing what they saw as brutal acts of repression against the Palestinian population was both a protest against the army's daily conduct in the occupied territories and a challenge to the legitimacy of the occupation. Their letter was intended to persuade Israeli Jews that unwarranted violence against civilians threatened Israel's very existence and eroded the Zionist principles in which they had been raised.

These Zionist principles to which the refuseniks referred are the moral, cultural, religious, and historical foundation that justifies the existence of Israel as a Jewish state and fosters Jewish national sentiment and national consciousness. This includes the Jews' right of return to what they consider the land of their biblical ancestors, as well as the creation of a safe harbor for the Jewish people. The complex meanings of Zionism have recently been the object of a heated debate in Israel, one that has caused many leading Israeli intellectuals to speak of a colonial thrust implicit in the Zionist project.

THE POLITICAL SETTING

There had been a precedent to this act of refusal. In 1982, when Israel invaded South Lebanon and was pushing toward Beirut, a group of Israeli soldiers protested. They formed a movement called Yesh Gvul,[3] maintaining that there is a limit to obeying orders when the lawful borders of their country were not being threatened. While these protesters were willing to fight for the defense of Israel, they were not prepared to take part in an elective war in which they were required to occupy Lebanese territories and attack civilians. As a result of their refusal to fight in Lebanon, 168 soldiers went to prison.

3. In Hebrew, "There is a limit (or border)."

The Yesh Gvul movement struck a chord in Israeli society, res-onating with a growing civil protest against a war deemed unnecessary and very costly for Israel. The sentiment exploded after Ariel Sharon, who was minister of defense at the time, not only gave the order to storm Beirut but also was implicated in the massacres of Sabra and Shatila.[4] The majority in Israel believed that Sharon's bellicose whim had cost the lives of hundreds of Israeli soldiers.

Yesh Gvul remained an active movement in Israel, picking up speed again during the first Intifada.[5] From 1987 to 1993, economic and humanitarian conditions in the occupied territories had been deterio-rating and had been further inflamed by an expansion of the settlements in the West Bank. Mass demonstrations, stone throwing, and riots were brutally put down by the Israeli Defense Forces. In all, 200 members of Yesh Gvul were imprisoned for refusing to fight against civilians in the occupied territories. Their message was clear: they would always defend their country, but they would not comply when service entailed committing acts of repression against civilians and occupying land they believed lay outside Israel's borders.[6]

After the 1993 Oslo Accords, however, the phenomenon of refusal all but vanished. For most Israelis, the signing of the accords meant the end of the occupation of the West Bank and Gaza Strip and the inevitable founding of a Palestinian State in the formerly occupied territories. The withdrawal of Israel from some Palestinian areas and the establishment

---

4. The 1982 massacres of Palestinians at the Sabra and Shatila refugee camps claimed the lives of at least 800 civilians, murdered by Lebanese Christian militiamen allied to Israel during its brief occupation of Beirut. The attack on the camps was part of an operation mounted by Sharon to eradicate what he saw as the terrorist threat posed by the Palestinians' military pres-ence in Lebanon.

5. Arabic for "uprising."

6. Though their refusal was met with fervent objections by the Israeli public, it nevertheless received support from some prominent intellectuals like the late Professor Yesha'ayahu Lei-bowitz. This Orthodox philosopher called on Israeli soldiers to adhere to their moral duty and refuse to use force against Palestinian civilians in the occupied territories. His grandson is one of the men interviewed in this book.

of the Palestinian Authority were perceived first and foremost as a wel-come separation from the Palestinian people. This meant that Israel was no longer responsible for the occupied territories: from now on, the Palestinian Authority would be in charge. At the time, all the soldiers who would later sign the refuseniks' letter believed that Israel was engaged in a peace process in good faith, and that an agreement with the Palestinians was in sight.

Yet the picture turned out to be different. Most of the territories remained under Israeli control. None of the subsequent Israeli govern-ments implemented the agreement signed in Oslo between Israel and the Palestinian Liberation Organization (PLO). After the assassination of Prime Minister Yitzhak Rabin in 1995, the Israeli government intensified a systematic policy of settlement expansion and constructed bypass roads dividing the territories into several separate areas. Indeed, more Palestinian land was expropriated and more settlements were built dur-ing Ehud Barak's tenure as prime minister (May 1999–February 2001) than during any previous administration.[7] The Palestinians were subject to closures that prevented them from working in Israel and earning a livelihood. They were not permitted to move freely inside the occupied territories.

In July 2000, the Palestinians rejected what was repeatedly described in the United States and Europe as "Ehud Barak's generous offer" (see Maps, Figure 8) at the Camp David Summit. Then, in Sep-tember of that year, Ariel Sharon visited the plaza outside the Al-Aqsa

7. Contrary to the expectations raised by the Oslo Accords, the government of Israel has implemented a systematic policy of settlement expansion. The number of housing units in the West Bank—not including East Jerusalem—and the Gaza Strip rose from 20,400 on the eve of the signing of the Declaration of Principles in September, 1993, to 32,800 in June, 2001. In other words, this was a 61% increase in less than eight years. The sharpest increase was regis-tered in the year 2000 during Ehud Barak's time as Prime Minister, where construction on some 4,800 new housing units was launched. At the end of 1993, the settler population in the West Bank—again, not including East Jerusalem—numbered 100,500. By the end of 2000, the pop-ulation had grown to 191,600, a 90% increase in a period of seven years. (B'tselem Settlement Report, 2000)

Mosque in East Jerusalem, one of the holiest places for Muslims. The visit was viewed as a provocation by Palestinians and Israeli doves alike.

On the first day of protests following the visit, the police killed nine Palestinians outside the Al-Aqsa Mosque. This marked the beginning of the second, or Al-Aqsa, Intifada. In the ensuing protests that erupted inside Israel, the police killed 13 Palestinian citizens of Israel. Responding to Israel's use of force against civilians in the occupied territories, Palestinians fired shells and bullets at Israeli soldiers and settlers. At this point, however, suicide bombers were not yet involved.

Sharon's visit was like a match set to a pile of hay: the frustration and anger caused by the continuing occupation and oppression had been accumulating and waiting for an outlet. The upheaval was crushed by closures, sieges, "eliminations" of suspected terrorists, and even shooting into crowds of protesters. By the time Ariel Sharon was elected in 2001, succeeding Barak, the trend toward increasingly brutal response to Palestinian attacks had already been established. As the repression escalated, the Palestinians became relentless and unyielding. Their hostility culminated in a massive wave of suicide bombings.[8] Israeli society was horrified. Anxiety gripped every citizen, and danger hung over every street.

Yesh Gvul inspired the Courage to Refuse movement, leading the protesters to hope that their letter would act as a wake-up call. In the past, the new refuseniks had never taken part in any organized noncompliance, nor did they belong to any radical political movements. But they now felt a strong need to persuade their fellow Israelis that the ongoing occupation did not serve a defensive purpose and was depriving Palestinians of their rights. They challenged the belief, widely held

8. Since the beginning of the Al-Aqsa Intifada, there has been a sharp increase in the number of attacks perpetrated by Palestinian organizations against Israeli civilians. These attacks have killed over 800 Israelis and wounded thousands, including many minors. Almost 2,000 Palestinians, likewise including many minors, have been killed by Israeli security forces' gunfire in the occupied territories.

in Israel, that their country had to protect itself in this way against Palestinian determination to get rid of the Zionist presence in the Middle East. Their message was that the occupation was illegal, and that its acts of humiliation and mistreatment were against their moral codes, codes that, for some of the refuseniks, were grounded in the religious and ethical precepts of Judaism.

They insisted that they had previously set out without hesitation to perform their duties in the occupied territories, in the belief that Israel was sincerely trying to bring an end to its occupation of the West Bank and the Gaza Strip. It was only after their experiences during the second Intifada that they felt compelled to refuse. Their letter was a desperate plea meant to show that, as Israeli patriots, they had no other choice.

The refusal came from respected members of the army, which is an important part of the Israeli mainstream, and the public's reaction to it was paradoxical: turmoil followed by rapid disappearance. For these reasons, it brought to the surface, perhaps for the first time since the creation of Israel, the conflicting ideals underlying the Zionist project. The issues it raised were of interest to me as an Israeli writer concerned with the political and cultural analysis of my society.

What did the refusal mean to these men? What were the different paths they took in reaching their decision? What does this act tell us about the assumptions shaping the awareness of Israelis today? With these questions in mind, I began conversations with nine participants in the refusenik movement in February 2002 and continued them over the course of several months.

What struck me most in my interaction with the refuseniks I met was that, from one conversation to the next, their political attitudes and their visions of Israel were undergoing a change. It became evident that, for them, it was one thing to make such a decision simply on moral

grounds, and quite another to deal with what they saw as the consequences of the Zionist project in light of the present situation in Israel.

Above all, the refuseniks I spoke with were determined to expose
the wrongdoings of the Israeli army. They insisted that their refusal was
a humanistic act and, when we began our talks, their main concern was
to share the depth of their patriotic commitment. It was only when they
started to reflect on the larger implications of this act that they brought
up questions about the ideology they believed to be pervasive in their
country. In the course of our conversations, the refuseniks gradually
came to wonder about the nature of social justice in Israel, including the
discrimination against Jews of Middle-Eastern origin and even more so
against Arab-Israeli citizens. The more they pondered the political consequences of their act, the more they became aware of the problems
that plague Israeli society.

THE SOCIOCULTURAL SETTING

For these male officers, being an Israeli citizen and a man meant being
a soldier, and indicting the Israeli army amounted to questioning an
essential part of their identity. Military service is the path to full membership in Israeli society: the army seals the relation between the citizens and the state.[9] Israeli-Jewish society is diverse, comprising Jews
of European origin, Jews from Arab countries, and more recent immigrants from Russia and Ethiopia. Although there is much tension
between the different groups, as well as between religious and nonre-
ligious Jews, serving in the armed forces eases many of these conflicts

---

9. Women must serve in the army for two years and may take part in combat if they so choose.
To date, only one woman soldier has publicly announced her refusal to serve in the occupied
territories. Military service is compulsory in Israel, but ultra-Orthodox groups have won
exemption for their women and their male religious students, a policy that has led to much
resentment in some quarters. Another group that does not serve, and is in any case marginalized in Israeli society, are the Arab citizens of the state.

through the process of forming a united consciousness devoted to the security and defense of the state. It is not surprising, therefore, that refusal to serve is considered an especially subversive act.

But the refuseniks did not perceive their declaration as a subversion of the system. They situated their actions within the ethos of the military: it was with their uniforms on that they made their plea to Israeli society. Their refusal sprang from the same roots as their willingness to sacrifice their lives for their country, and they proudly maintain that they are an integral part of the army and of Israeli society. Moreover, they had been meeting with the men in their units for a month of reserve duty every year and shared important experiences with them. Leaving their comrades-in-arms was often more painful than a jail sentence.[10]

They also made it abundantly clear that they were ready to serve under any circumstances, except when it came to enforcing the occupation. They insisted on the distinction between defending Israel within the borders established after the 1948 War of Independence and maintaining its illegitimate occupation of the land seized after the 1967 war.

Most of the refuseniks I spoke with live in Tel Aviv or Jerusalem. They were raised within the Israeli establishment and constitute quite a homogenous social group. In their 30s and 40s, good looking, well spoken, and self-confident, most of them are professionals. Many earned university degrees, and some hold important jobs: professor, lawyer, film-maker, and the like. They are the cream of the crop. Since most of them are Ashkenazim,[11] this group has enjoyed high social status in Israel and has traditionally set the tone on the political and cultural scene. In other words, the refuseniks had never felt marginal—and so

10. Not all refuseniks go to prison automatically. Some have been offered alternative military duties in which they will not be required to serve in the occupied territories. In other cases, the army has avoided court-martialing the soldiers so as not to publicize their cause, preferring instead to give the men disciplinary hearings before their commanding officers. In these cases, the prison sentences have ranged from 14 to 35 days, whereas in a court martial the sentences could range from 1 to 3 years.

11. Jews of Western origin.

they were stunned when they realized that their message had been dismissed by the Israeli public. The values and beliefs of their own social and cultural milieu, it turned out, had became the first target of their act.

Initially, the letter received widespread attention and caused an unprecedented debate. The refuseniks were interviewed for weekend supplements of leading newspapers and appeared on many television programs. Articles about the movement were published daily in op-ed sections, especially in *Ha'aretz*. Most of the columnists objected to the refuseniks' letter, yet some of them felt obliged to address the protesters' concerns. The result was that the issue of occupation became part of public debate as never before.

The reason for this impressive reception, at least for a short time, was that Israeli society could not easily dismiss the call of its most revered members, these much-respected combat officers. Once the men broke ranks, however, the army felt free to express its contempt. It used several different tactics against the refuseniks. To begin with, it claimed that refusing to serve was not only unacceptable but also disgraceful. Then it argued that Courage to Refuse was a marginal phenomenon of no consequence. Some army unit commanders made public statements to the effect that, under their leadership, the atrocities described by the refuseniks had never taken place. The refusenik officers were accused of being traitors, or at best victims of propaganda. Eventually, a decision was made by the Chief of Staff to ignore them and thus erase them from all public debates.

Attacks against them did not come only from the right-wing circles that are traditionally the most ardent supporters of the military. Right-wing representatives did indeed insist that the refuseniks be severely punished: one rabbi from the settlements stated that they should be killed. Yet representatives of Meretz, the liberal party, also condemned them. Although some of its members remained ambivalent, the official position of Meretz was highly critical.[12]

Two arguments coming from the peace camp proved especially challenging for the refuseniks. First, they were accused of establishing a dangerous precedent. After all, should the time come to evacuate the settlements in the West Bank and the Gaza Strip, soldiers sympathetic to the cause of the settlers could be tempted to similar acts of disobedience. What would the country do if a new, right-wing refusenik movement suddenly appeared?

Second, many critics claimed that the refuseniks made a serious mistake by leaving their military posts to people less sensitive to humanitarian issues. These principled refuseniks, the argument went, were precisely the kind of soldiers who could prevent heartless actions. Their refusal was seen as an abandonment of their responsibilities: they should have remained on duty and kept their protest confined to the political arena.

The refuseniks did not dismiss these accusations, but they felt a need to set the record straight. The arguments they used and the examples they gave seemed to be addressed chiefly to their severest critics, with whom they felt they could identify, since, before their act of refusal, they had shared the same set of cultural assumptions. The refuseniks stirred up a debate they themselves had not anticipated. But soon new events pushed this nascent discussion aside. A series of terrorist attacks shook Israel, and violence escalated. The atmosphere changed, and the refuseniks' cause was promptly forgotten. The press now

12. At the beginning of the second Intifada, Meretz was part of Ehud Barak's coalition and supported his policy in the occupied territories. Meretz describes itself as a peace-seeking party, committed to human rights, equality, social justice, Israel's security, and the values of humane Zionism.

focused exclusively on the Palestinian suicide bombers, adding to the pervasive sense of panic.

On March 27, 2002, Passover night, a suicide bomb exploded at the Park Hotel in the coastal town of Netanya.[13] Two days later, Operation Defensive Shield was launched in retaliation. At the onset of the operation, reserve soldiers were mobilized en masse. Their growing enthusiasm for joining the war against terrorism further stigmatized the refuseniks' cause.

In Israel it became much more difficult to defend the position of refusal. After the first few weeks following the publication of their letter, the refuseniks found that they had been dismissed. While the foreign press reported on their activities, including a "60 Minutes" program in the United States on May 5, 2002, and many small demonstrations and conventions were organized throughout Israel and Europe to support their cause, the Israeli press remained conspicuously silent. The refuseniks had failed in their attempt to convince the public, and especially their fellow soldiers, that, no matter what Israel claimed, intensifying the repression of uprisings in the West Bank and Gaza would not put an end to terrorist attacks.

At this point, an interesting shift occurred. The refuseniks' voice had been silenced by the Israeli media and had thus to all intents and purposes vanished from official notice. And yet, within a month after Operation Defensive Shield began, the numbers of refuseniks started rising, bringing the membership in Courage to Refuse up to 489.[14]

13. Twenty-eight people were killed.

14. Some refuseniks belong to other organizations like Yesh Gvul and New Profile, and some are independent, with the total membership being over 1,000. In addition, on September 17, 2002, 210 young women and men, high-school seniors, sent a letter to Prime Minister Ariel Sharon, with copies to the minister of education, minister of defense, and chief of staff, declaring that they would "refuse to be soldiers of the occupation." Of every annual group of candidates for military service in Israel, at least one third fails to enlist altogether. Around another 15 percent leave the service early on. As a result, full military service is performed by only half of every annual cohort. In other words, alongside the openly declared resistance, a "silent resistance" is taking place as well.

The combat soldiers' letter was written 15 months after the second Intifada began and a few months before the Israeli army reentered the cities that had been handed over to the Palestinian Authority as part of the Oslo Accords. This was the time when Israel had started to intensify its military occupation, deliberately destroying the Palestinian social infrastructure: the water supply, sewer systems, schools, hospitals, cultural centers, and the like, which had been in the making since 1994.[15] These soldiers serving in the occupied territories had come to the reluctant realization that they could no longer trust the legitimacy of orders coming from above.[16] Though they had cherished the ideals of Zionism, the refuseniks began to wonder how the Jewish state could justify the occupation of a land inhabited by over 3 million Palestinians. A solution must be found, they claimed, to ensure the Palestinians their rights without jeopardizing the existence of Israel.

In the process of struggling to understand the meaning of their act of refusal, these men gradually began to question their compatriots' perception of reality. The refuseniks came to challenge the consensual notion that placed all blame for the growing violence on the Palestinians, thereby legitimizing what they viewed as the policy of oppression initiated by Barak and continued by Sharon. Could it be, they started asking, that Palestinian malevolence was not the sole source of the problem? Could it be that Israel too bore responsibility for the escalation of violence and the loss of lives?

The refuseniks have emphatically pointed out that Israel cannot simply wish the Palestinian problem away, and that it will certainly not disappear through what they see as a policy of starvation, aerial bom-

15. The Oslo Accords were signed in 1993. In 1994 the Palestinian Authority, returning to the West Bank and Gaza from Tunis, became operative in the cities from which Israel withdrew.
16. Months later, their case appeared close to a legal resolution in the Israeli High Court. However, on December 30, 2002, the High Court ruled that reservists in the IDF did not have the right to refuse their orders to serve in the West Bank and Gaza. The High Court determined that recognizing selective conscientious objection would turn the IDF "into an army with every unit having its own conscience, which will determine how it can operate."

bardment, closure, demolition, widespread humiliation, and killing. Nevertheless, beyond questioning the political consequences of Zionist ideals, these protesters have been at a loss to think of alternative visions of the future.

This "blank" shared by all those who sincerely wish for a peaceful settlement between Israel and the Palestinians may well be at the root of the present drama in the Middle East. Why is it so difficult to create an imaginary space for a new society in which both peoples can live side by side as equals? If such an idea could at least be conceived in the minds of both Israelis and Palestinians, reconciliation and forgiveness might be more than just a dream.

CHAPTER ONE

Sergeant First Class (Res.) Assaf Oron

The following letter was written by one of the refuseniks, Assaf Oron, in response to a wave of vehement protests by the Jewish community in the United States following the Tikkun organization's full-page announcement in the *New York Times* supporting the refuseniks. It establishes why their cause is not merely a local Israeli issue, and it addresses the meaning of the Jewish collectivity. (The letter has been edited and revised for its publication in this book.)

AN OPEN LETTER TO AMERICAN JEWS AND FRIENDS OF ISRAEL WORLDWIDE

Dear People,

Yesterday I was informed of an interesting phenomenon: a peace-supporting Jewish organization called Tikkun published an ad in our favor, expressing their support for the Israeli-reservist refuseniks. They were immediately bombarded with hate mail and phone calls from other Jews. What's more interesting is that even the Jews who consider themselves supporters of peace have denounced the Tikkun ad. Some Tikkun Advisory Board members resigned to minimize any personal damage to themselves. This has so saddened, disturbed, and angered me that I find myself setting aside half a day on the eve of Passover to write this open letter.

Most of these "civilized" attacks, so I understand, were aimed at this or that detail of the Tikkun ad. Here in Israel, in the past two months since we published our own open letter to the Israeli public in favor of refusal, I've also heard many arguments about the specifics of our acts. The general theme is the issue of tribalism. A loud voice (and in Israel today a loud voice is the only voice allowed to be heard) keeps shouting that we are in the midst of a war between two tribes: a tribe of human beings, of pure good—the Israelis—and a tribe of subhumans, of pure evil—the Palestinians. Only one tribe will survive. Even if we are not purely good, we must put morality and conscience to sleep. We must shut up and fight to kill. Otherwise the Palestinians will throw us into the sea.

Does this ring a bell for you? It does for me. As a child growing up in Israel, all I heard was that the Arabs were inhuman monsters, that they understood only force, and that, ever since the IDF won the Six Day War, they knew not to mess with us anymore. And, of course, we had to keep the "liberated" territories in our hands. Then came the Yom Kippur War. For a child of 7, it was the perfect proof that indeed the Arabs wanted to throw us into the sea. What a great opportunity it was for our glorious IDF to teach them a lesson. I was too young to evaluate how the war really ended. All the ceasefires and talks were too complicated and boring, far more boring than war.

A few years went by, and a funny thing happened: those "we'll throw you into the sea" Arabs came to talk peace. In exchange for all of Sinai, they were willing to sign a full peace agreement. Already a teenager, I went and protested against the withdrawal from Sinai. After all, it was a purely logical issue: the Arabs were not to be trusted; that's what we'd been taught from day one.

But the "throw us into the sea" paradigm immediately found new arenas. The reality of the northern border was unpleasant. Even though the forces on the other side had strictly adhered to a secret cease-fire agreement for about a year, they were Arabs and therefore could not be trusted. So we talked ourselves into invading Lebanon and setting up a friendlier regime there. The mastermind of the invasion was then-Minister of Defense Ariel Sharon. Shimon Peres, the head of the opposition at the time, voted together with his party in favor of the invasion. For me, at 16, this was also a turning point. When I understood that the government had lied to me in order to sell me this war, I turned from "center-right" to being a leftist. Sadly enough, it has taken me almost 20 more years, in a slow and painful process, to understand how deeply these lies and delusions are rooted in our shared perception of reality.

When Peres withdrew most of our forces from Lebanon in 1985, the Arabs could still not be trusted. To soothe our endless paranoia and suspicion, we created that perpetual source of death and crime ironically called the "security zone." It took many years, a lot of blood, and Four Mothers[1] against almost all politicians, generals, and columnists to finally pull us out of Lebanon.

As for the Palestinians, they are painfully close to us. Like rival siblings, we have singled them out for hostility. We perfected our treatment of them in that strange no-man's-land created in 1967 and now known as "the territories." We have created an entirely hallucinatory reality, in which the true humans, members of the nation of masters, could move and settle freely and safely, while the subhumans, the nation of slaves, were shoved into the corners, kept invisible, and controlled under our IDF boots.

I know. I've been there. I was taught how to do this, back in the mid-1980s. I did it, and I was witness to deeds that I'm ashamed to remember to this day.

---

1. An Israeli women's movement that called for unilateral Israeli withdrawal from Lebanon.

When a fledgling and hesitant peace process tried to work its way through this mess, one major factor (perhaps *the* factor) that undermined it and voided it of meaning was our establishment's endless fear and suspicion of the Other. To resolve this fear and suspicion, we chose the insane route of demanding full control of the Other throughout the process. When this Other finally decided that we were cheating him of his freedom (and had too many mental disorders of his own to accommodate ours as well), violence erupted, and all our ancient instincts woke up. There they are. Now we see their true face again, we said in relief. The Arabs want to throw us into the sea. There's no one to talk with, there is "no partner," in the words of our beloved ex-prime minister,[2] and they understand only force. And so we responded with more and more and more force, so they would know not to mess with us anymore. It was like putting out a fire with a barrel of gasoline. And that's the moment when I said to myself, "That's it, I'm not playing this game anymore."

But what about the threat to our existence, you may ask. Well, I ask you, don't you have eyes? Don't you see our tanks rolling into Palestinian streets every other day? Don't you see our helicopters hovering over their neighborhoods, choosing which window to shoot a missile into? What type of security need are we answering by trampling down the Palestinians?

Prevention of terror, I hear you say. What a joke.

We have sown the seeds, grown them, and nurtured them. And then our blood is spilled, and the centrist-right-wing politicians reap the benefits. Indeed, terror is the right-wing politician's best friend. You know what? When you treat millions of people like subhumans for so long, some of them will adopt inhuman strategies to fight back. Isn't that what the Zionists and other Jewish revolutionaries argued about a hundred years ago in order to explain the questionable strate-

2. Israeli Prime Minister Ehud Barak, who served from 1999 to 2001.

gies of survival that Jews used in Europe? Didn't our forefathers say, "Let us live like human beings, and see how we'll act just like other human beings"?

I hope that the first part of this letter made it clear that I don't buy the "they want to throw us into the sea" argument. It's a delusion of ours. More important, I don't see the world in tribal terms. I see people, human beings. I believe that the Palestinians are human beings like us. We must treat them as human beings without demanding anything in return. And to all die-hard Barak fans, I say that throwing the Palestinians a couple of crumbs to set up pitiful, completely controlled Bantustans between our settlements and bypass roads, and believing this to be a great act of generosity, does not come close to answering this basic requirement. This requirement is not negotiable. In a perfect demonstration of historical justice, it is a vital requirement for the survival of our own state.

Based on the lessons of modern history, especially the history of the Arab–Israeli conflict, I believe that the Palestinians will find calm, and that the elusive "security and peace" will finally happen for us as they did, incidentally, for almost two whole years between the Wye Plantation Accord of 1998 and Camp David 2000. I don't have any insurance policy for that, except the solemn promise of the entire Arab world. In any case, we see now what the opposite paradigm ensures us.

In the meantime, I refuse to be a terrorist in my tribe's name. That's what this is, not a "war against terror," as our propaganda machine tries to persuade us. This is a war of terror. In retaliation for Palestinian guerrilla warfare and terror, we employ the IDF in two types of terror. The more visible one is the violence of killing and destruction, which some people still try to explain away as surgical acts of defense though they result in the acceleration of conflict and bloodshed. The worse type of terror is the silent one, which has continued unabated since 1967 and through the entire Oslo process. It is the ter-ror of occupation, of humiliation on a personal and collective basis, of deprivation and legalized robbery, of alternating exploitation and star-vation. This is the base of the iceberg.

I live in terrible fear of the moment our government will sense a "blackout" situation, a huge terror attack, an American attack on Iraq, and there will be a horrible bloodbath in the territories, compared to which the last year and a half will look like a picnic.

I would like to dedicate a few lines to an unavoidable issue: the Nazi allusion. There is a great deal of self-righteousness and hypocrisy on the part of those Israelis who complain that a parallel is drawn between Israeli and Nazi behavior. Parties that support the essentially Nazi idea of deporting all Palestinians from the country have been part of our Knesset and our "legitimate" political map since 1984. Recent opinion polls show that 35 to 45 percent of the Jewish public currently supports this "solution," as it is sometimes called. Last weekend, Reserve General Effi Eitam, fresh out of the military and ready to take up the leadership of the national-religious movement, was the subject of a flattering cover story in the *Ha'aretz* weekend supplement. He unfolded his chilling ideology, calling for the expulsion as serfs to Jor-dan of those Palestinians who don't want to remain in the Galilee and West Bank, and as the same from Gaza to Sinai. And he basically said: Why should we, the country poorest in natural resources, bear the bur-den of solving the Palestinian problem? That recalls some of the Nazi rhetoric in that dark period between the Kristallnacht of 1938 and the beginning of the war, when the Jews were expelled from Germany but could find no safe haven anywhere else. When I see a retired IDF gen-eral and rising political star use the exact same Nazi rhetoric in what is considered Israel's most liberal newspaper, without any criticism by his interviewer or the editors, my hair stands up in horror.

Some two months ago, around January 25th, one of the top commanders in the territories was quoted in *Ha'aretz* as saying that, in order to prepare for potential battles in dense urban neighborhoods, the IDF must learn, if necessary, how the German army "operated" in the Warsaw Ghetto. A week later, the reporter confirmed the quote and the fact that it was a widespread opinion in the IDF, and then he went as far as to defend it on moral grounds. Again, this was published in *Ha'aretz* without a hint of criticism. Beyond the disgust these sentiments evoke, we soon found that they were not spoken in vain. A few weeks later, the IDF found an excuse to invade a refugee camp: an incontestable and inexcusable war crime. At the height of the invasion, we were hit with a series of bloody retaliatory suicide bombings. And lo and behold: the IDF high command patted itself on the back morally and professionally, claiming that these invasions prevented terrorism and merely killed dozens instead of thousands. In fact, the primary reason behind the limited carnage was the responsible decision taken by the "terrorists" not to turn the camps into all-out battlefields. But this could change in the next round.

I have little hope that the Israeli public will wake up and stop this escalation of violence. In their fear and confusion aided by politicians and the mass media, the Israelis have made a decision to go back to sleep and wake up only after it is all over. But it won't be over. While the mind sleeps, our muscles tighten the nightmarish death grip. The only sensible thing is to let go, and that requires an open mind. Will you join the hypocritical mobs that sing lullabies to Israel and pounce upon anyone who tries to wake her up? Or will you finally take responsibility and be the true friends that Israel needs now, even if this means not being "nice" to Israel for awhile?

Tonight, remember more than one thousand people, three quarters of them Palestinian and one quarter of them Israeli, who were here with us a year ago and who were murdered.[3] Most of them could have been here with us today if we had acted sooner. We have now done what little we can. I beg you to think of the many thousands who may be doomed if you continue to sit on the fence. Please help us struggle to be free from fear, racism, hatred, and the deaths they produce.

Yours,
Assaf Oron

---

3. A few days after the letter was written, Israel invaded and reconquered the Palestinian cities. More people have been killed on both sides in the months that followed than from the beginning of the Intifada in October 2000.

Assaf Oron is a fair-skinned man with curly hair and eyes that fluctuate between blue and green. At 36, this father of two works as a developer with a start-up company and lives in Moshav Nehora in southern Israel. He grew up in the posh neighborhood of Beit Ha-Kerem in Jerusalem, and now he serves humanitarian campaigns for Palestinians who have been rendered homeless, hungry, and in need of medical attention after Israeli military operations. An active member of the refusenik movement, he objects to the occupation and declares his solidarity with the victims of excessive Israeli military force.

I met Assaf Oron in April 2001 on the road to Ramallah, where some 3,000 men and women, Palestinians and Jews, were holding a demonstration at a checkpoint. The crowd came out to express their identification with the besieged residents of Ramallah. At the time, Israeli soldiers were conducting house-to-house searches of the city. To this end, they effectively placed entire families, including children and the elderly, under house arrest for hours on end. In the streets, pedestrians scrambled to the grocery store, fearful of the crackle of gunfire and the arbitrary whims of snipers during day after day of curfew. Weeks of military bombardments had denied the residents of the city access to medical services, running water, electricity, and phone service. The siege exposed the population to humiliation, torment, looting, vandalism, and the calculated eradication of the infrastructure that provided their subsistence. The protesters expressed their solidarity with the people of Ramallah, and they intended to deliver truckloads of food and medicine to them. The demonstration met with violent retaliation. The army surrounded the protesters and shot stun grenades and tear gas into the crowd until they dispersed.

Many of the refuseniks will not participate in such demonstrations. They consider these protests too radical to the extent that they express solidarity with the Palestinians. As a result, the great extent of refusenik activism remains within the limits of Israeli public discourse. Assaf Oron cannot be confined within those boundaries. He is driven by an urge to cross the lines and to demonstrate solidarity outside his camp.

Similarly, the story of his upbringing demonstrates the inherent contradictions in Israeli society. Assaf's mother demonstrated against the 1982 Sabra and Shatila massacres in Lebanon in the cause of humanism. His father, a military man, is thoroughly convinced that the entire world is out to get Israel, and that only naked force will prevent this from happening.

They are not an unusual couple in Israel. There is family tension between the side that wants to reach out to the world, including the Arabs, and the other side that has no such trust. The same ambivalence met Assaf Oron's refusal to serve in the occupation. His mother demonstrated cautious sympathy, while his father took offense. By and large, the positions that women and men assume in such instances occur in accordance with the roles assigned to them in Israeli society.

Assaf Oron's conduct revealed this contradiction. He continued to serve in a unit that, he felt, violated the very human rights he struggled to defend as a volunteer at Hotline for the Defense of the Individual. Here we see the internal paradox of Israeli humanism. You can carve out a small space in your life to answer humanitarian needs without shirking the one responsibility society expects most of you: military service. Assaf's story, as he related it to me, chronicles his crises of conscience and how he met these challenges with both weakness and strength.

———

ORON: I was raised on my father's tirades against the left. Since he was a lieutenant colonel and a career officer, he believes that Israel's strength lies in its military might. He is also a refugee whose politics are informed by his own persecution and reverence for power.

When my father was 2 years old, he lived in a shtetl in Poland. There the Russians turned to the Jews and said, "Run, or the Germans will kill you." So my father and his family escaped eastward, loading the few possessions they could gather onto army carts. In this way, they sat out the remainder of the war all alone in the northern regions of Russia. My grandparents' world was devastated. After the war they came to Israel. Supposedly, my father blended into Israeli society, but his identity as a refugee dominates his worldview.

My mother's background is different. She was raised in a liberal Central European home. Before the war, her mother left the area later known as Auschwitz and came to Palestine as a pioneer. She belonged to a privileged group. They had the money to obtain the permits required to emigrate to Palestine.

On the one hand, I grew up with my father's hawkish ideas: a deep feeling that the State of Israel is a replay of the Warsaw Ghetto uprising. Only this time, we are going to win. On the other hand, I was raised on universal morality and peace, freedom, justice, and equality for all. While we listened to peace songs by Lennon, Dylan, and Bob Marley, we also reveled in those songs where a girl drives a tank at sunset through the fields: "The tank is yours/and you are ours." So I was raised in two different value systems: a moral code and a tribal code. I thought they were compatible. But the occupation has deformed our tribal code to the point that it contradicts our moral code.

At 18, I entered the army. I didn't join out of enthusiasm. I did what everyone did. I tried not to stand out. Where else can you parade around feeling like a hero protecting the homeland as you harass passers-by, humiliate them as you please, and joke about it with the guys? They didn't tell us to torment people, but they did tell us to be harsh. Our job was to give the Palestinians a hard time, especially the young people. They were always under suspicion.

Without thinking and without feeling, I became belligerent. Once we detained a guy, and he escaped. We chased him. Then we started beating him in an orchard.

At the end of the summer of 1987, the twilight of the "enlightened occupation" before the first Intifada, a Palestinian detainee was loaded into our command car somewhere around Tulkarm. He sat on the floor, blindfolded, with his hands tied behind his back. A fellow soldier sat across from me. While smiling straight at me, he landed a blow to the detainee's head. I didn't say a word. I was the platoon sergeant, the highest-ranking soldier in the vehicle. Then came another blow. I could have stopped the beating, but I didn't do a thing. I had already lost my soul. In Qalqilya, I myself had slapped people just for being insolent. The detainee only got a few blows to the head, but the memory of that beating will never leave mine.

Another time, I tore up the identity cards of men my father's age. I beat people, I harassed them, and I did all this in Qalqilya, in western Samaria, the northern area of the West Bank, five kilometers from the warm and cozy home of my grandparents. I wasn't an exception. I was perfectly ordinary. As a sergeant and a field officer, I set the example.

My service in western Samaria left me with a sense of destitution. The Jewish settlements there looked like a nightmare. Skeletons of unfinished houses were scattered in the middle of nowhere. Israeli real estate agents had come to buy land from Palestinians and sell it to Jews. Sometimes the land was never really purchased, or it was purchased from Palestinians who didn't own it. The contractors took the money from clients who had paid for the villa of their dreams, on rocky hills, and then fled abroad. The ugly, half-built houses stayed behind. The settlements looked disjointed and barren. There was something so contrived in that construction boom. The architecture and abandoned gardens stood at odds with some cute, freshly built houses with red roofs and well-tended gardens. These villas crept down onto Arab villages where people burned cow dung and had nothing to eat. And the residents of these villas wondered why their neighbors broke into their homes.

I sensed something was wrong, but I repressed it. Only later did I start asking questions. When I was a student in 1990, a friend took me to volunteer with him at the Hotline for the Defense of the Individual, an organization that deals with human-rights violations in the occupied territories. I was curious to know what was happening on the Palestinian side.

Exposed to human-rights violations in East Jerusalem and the territories, I started to see the army from the other side. I started to understand just how unacceptable our military's conduct was. The hotline staff split into two groups, the leftists and an apolitical group. I belonged to the apolitical group that wanted to deal with human rights. I found myself working in a small, crowded, smoke-filled room in East Jerusalem, burrowing through files about death, torture, bureaucratic wickedness, or simple daily mistreatment. I felt as though I were atoning for my actions in Givati.[4] But I also felt as though I were emptying the sea with a teaspoon.

I learned how systematic human-rights violations in the territories are, and how the judicial system does somersaults to allow the abuse of Palestinian civilians without explicitly sanctioning it. The daily life of Palestinians is determined by our belief that everything falls under the rubric of battle. Even private life is part of this battle. That's why civil rights are disregarded. It's a zero-sum game, in which their benefit means our loss. The objective is to embitter the Palestinians, to prevent them from conducting normal lives, to toy with them,

---

4. An elite infantry corps involved in combat operations on the ground.

to remind them constantly who's in charge. For example, people who wanted permission to travel abroad were asked to collaborate with the army or sign a declaration that they wouldn't return for years.

We prepared a report about travel permits. I assumed that people would read it and understand what was happening, that the goal was to reduce the number of young men in the territories to as few as possible. No one cared. Nobody wanted to know. My friends didn't take an interest. People asked me, "Why are you helping Arabs? Don't we have enough problems?"

My three consecutive periods of reserve duty in the territories turned into a routine of nausea and shame. I became a closet conscientious objector. I asked to guard the post, to man the radio on a far-away hill, to patrol forgotten settlements, whatever excuse I could find. I was ashamed to tell the guys why I preferred guard-duty to going into the field with them. I didn't have the energy to be chided about being a bleeding heart. I was ashamed because it was an easy way out. I was ashamed all the way around. But I saved my soul. I didn't participate in wrongdoing. Why didn't I refuse altogether? I was afraid to break ranks. The peace process also gave me a glimmer of hope that the whole wretched affair would soon be behind us.

But I also saw how the army quietly and purposefully sabotages the Oslo Accords by creating pockets of resistance. I understood this from our commander's orders. For instance, a few days before the withdrawal from Bethlehem, I was on reserve duty in the area. The mood was festive, with a consensus among leftist and right-wing soldiers about the Bethlehem hand-over. But our orders were, "Patrol the mosques, where the fanatics are, and get their names." It was clear that the commanders didn't understand we were out of there.

In 1997 I did my reserve duty in Gaza. I couldn't believe what was happening. In theory, Gaza had been given back to the Palestinians, but the occupation continued in full force. The people were captives, allowed neither entry nor exit. I knew such an imprisoned population was a ticking time-bomb. But Barak set the timer during the first few weeks of the current Intifada. True, Sharon's infamous visit to the Al-Aqsa mosque caused demonstrations with stone throwing and burning tires, but the Israeli response with live ammunition was entirely out of proportion. They positioned snipers on roofs and started eliminating people.

It was obvious that the security forces had so much pent-up fury that it was just waiting to be unleashed. The same is true for the Palestinians, but our side is immeasurably advantaged in terms of weaponry. Later on, they started assassinating people from helicopters, as well.

Until then, execution units like Duvdevan[5] had walked the Palestinian streets in civilian clothing and done what no one wants to talk about. Once, this dubious work of assassination was considered depraved. Now soldiers think it's the apex of action. People stand in line to get into those units. But when gunships shoot people from the air, they kill women and children along with wanted men.

In Barak's October 2000 speech, in which he stated that he had no negotiating partner, he primed the public for the escalation of violence we see now. That very night, Jews launched pogroms against Arabs in Tiberias, Nazareth, and Jaffa.[6] Then it became clear to me that I wasn't willing to fight this war. I decided to refuse.

In January 2002, when I came to the first refusers' meeting, it was as if I looked in the mirror and saw twenty reflections of myself. Socially speaking, we all came from the same place. We were good

---

5. A special operations unit in the IDF, with the code name literally translated as "Cherry." This squad, established in the 1980s, specialized in pretending to be Palestinians. In the 1990s they became a killing squad.

6. After Barak's speech, a perception spread that the peace process had failed. Arab-Israelis identifying with the Palestinian cause protested on a large scale. Enmity between Arab and Jewish citizens reached a peak, not only because of the sporadic acts of violence that Oron mentions, but also because of the use by police of live ammunition at demonstrations in which 13 young Arabs were shot dead.

middle-class kids. Maybe I can allow myself to rebel because I take it for granted that I live comfortably. Perhaps the ability to rebel is related to one's proximity to Zionism. Those who didn't grow up with the assumption that their parents and grandparents were full partners in the Zionist project must find it harder to contradict the state.

The people who can make a bold move at a given moment are those who are not constrained economically, culturally, or socially. That's why those who grew up in the elite and have the power to impact things have a responsibility to change the face of society. We are obligated to do something about it. The onus is on us to be the straw that breaks the occupation's back, so to speak. Only then can we salvage a future for the inhabitants of this land.

CHACHAM: In April 2002, during Operation Defensive Shield, the Israeli army besieged Arafat's compound and reoccupied the Palestinian cities and refugee camps of the West Bank. At that time, I spoke with someone who was contemplating refusal. The soldier said he knew he was about to receive an emergency call-to-arms. He knew that he might die for something he didn't believe in, but what could he tell his brothers and friends who were already there? He didn't believe that military operations would bring about anything desirable. He was aware, he said, of the demagogy of the state's assertion that the Palestinians stand before us ready to destroy us. He assumed that the state needed people to sacrifice themselves. Finally, he knew that only when soldiers started coming home in coffins would public opinion change. Still, he found it impossible not to stand in solidarity with his brothers and friends.

ORON: I identify with his feelings. The most difficult thing is to break ranks. But once you become aware that what you're doing is a crime, that barrier is removed. From his perspective, the Palestinians' situation is irrelevant. What the army does to Palestinians doesn't seem to factor into his decision-making process, unfortunately.

There's a whole culture built around not getting into politics. It's an ideology based on the idea, "Don't worry about your conscience, worry about your career." And always look for the comfortable, easy solution. At most, you can demonstrate in the town square. But to transfer food to starving Palestinians, to demonstrate solidarity with Arabs, to break away from the pack? That's too much.

CHACHAM: I want to present you with more claims made against refusal. There are those who posit that it's important that there be officers in the army who will ensure that soldiers behave humanely, and that in light of that, refusal is just an indulgence.

One of your opponents gave me an example regarding firing regulations. Lately, these regulations have become far more lenient. For example, now a soldier is allowed to shoot at the legs of anyone who throws a stone. But if a commander does not issue such an order to his soldiers, the order will not be carried out. It's the commander's prerogative.

I also heard tell of operations that can be executed in a humane fashion—for example, shaking down a village where stones are repeatedly being thrown. A shakedown means making the adults' lives just miserable enough to get them to curb the youth from throwing stones. It's not awful. It's not horrendous. It's about making a lot of noise. Conducting searches for no reason. Entering homes.

And then, this same opponent told me, "You see the children and the mothers and your heart breaks. But when you see a female settler hit with a rock, your heart breaks too." According to him, the soldiers do it because there's no other choice. But they try to treat the children with kindness. They put candy in their pockets to hand out to the kids.

ORON: I hardly have the energy to respond. At best, whoever says such things is covering up the truth. There's no way to act humane in such circumstances. I don't understand how you can impose a curfew humanely.

Take the story of the 2-year-old baby, Tabarak Odeh, from a village near Nablus. She needed medicine just to survive. Her village was under curfew, and her parents ran out of medicine. The army forbade anyone to bring in medicine or food. After a few days, the baby died. I became involved in this case. Various Palestinian organizations appealed to everyone but could not obtain permission to take the baby to the hospital. When they asked Israeli peace activists to intervene, it finally worked, but by then it was too late.

This is the story of one baby. The doctor at the Nablus hospital told me, "There are many others like her in need of medical attention whom we can't reach." The soldier at the checkpoint who received the orders not to let ambulances through was just doing his job. He didn't mean to cause Tabarak's death. But will someone please answer me: When you halt ambulances, aren't you the one who is indulging yourself to believe that you aren't killing babies?

As for the example of shaking down a village, why does the rhetoric about collective punishment sound so cool-headed? We forget how it resonates with the practices of the most despicable regimes. Democracies don't punish people collectively. It's a crime.

CHACHAM: But how do you deal with the fact that the majority of the Israeli public is convinced that we are in a no-choice situation? It may be that what Israel's doing in the territories isn't moral, but how can that be avoided? The suicide bombings must be averted at any cost, even if at the expense of morality.

ORON: How can such blind faith be shattered? Suicide bombings are the oil that fuels Sharon's fire, and his tank is always full. Every time we experience a period of relative calm, he assassinates someone, and the bombings start again. Suicide bombings serve his interest in avoiding the possibility of reaching an agreement with the Palestinians. They could have restored a border and patrolled that border, but that would have left the settlers on the wrong side of the fence.

Even the settlers are willing to sacrifice all of Israel for their own interests. With every new bombing, they reap the political benefits. I don't think they rejoice when someone explodes in the center of the country, but it definitely serves their interests.

In the name of our patriotism, we need international protection. When I say this, I'm attacked for ignoring the suicide bombings. But I say, "Come protect us, because our government is not doing what it should to save us from suicide bombings." My patriotism is for both peoples. As for convincing people that we do have a partner to talk with, I don't get how the Israeli public buys the story about the Palestinian Authority being responsible for everything, while Israel does whatever it can to disable their capacity to rule.

So many lies are being disseminated. Consider all the years they've talked about the refugee camps. They've always said, "Why don't the Arabs resolve the problem of the miserable refugees? Because they want to use them in their propaganda about the suffering of the Palestinian people." Israel has continuously made this claim about the Arab states. According to the Geneva Conventions, the occupier must ensure the welfare of the people under its control. Israel has never bothered to improve the refugees' living conditions and has never given them aid. The refugees have received all their help from international organizations.

Not only have the refugee camps received nothing from Israel, neither have the Palestinian villages and towns inside the Green Line. Has Israel provided construction for the Palestinian citizens of Israel? Since the establishment of the state, all Israel has done is rob them of their lands and discriminate against them in every aspect of civil life.

And now you have the story in Jenin.[7] It's clear that there was a cover-up.

What happened in Jenin reinforced my feeling that I was brought up on lies and that everything needs to be reexamined, because I'm continually discovering new ones. Over the last few weeks, I've seen the Jenin survivors wandering aimlessly without any possessions, searching hopelessly for a remnant of their lives. They're collecting handwritten lists of names, trying to figure out who is there, who is missing, who is alive, and who God-knows-what. They're trying to salvage something, and more importantly someone, with their bare hands, with their nails, without anybody's help.

And mighty, technological Israel, which never misses a chance to show its stuff in international search-and-rescue efforts, is doing nothing at all. Instead, Israel is dragging this horrific situation out day after day, trying to buy time, hoping to eradicate any trace of what happened there.

This is a life-or-death battle against corruption. We must expose the naked brutality behind all this. We must struggle. And, in order to prevail, we must be ready to break through mental and emotional barriers.

---

7. On April 3, 2002, the Israeli Defense Forces launched a major military operation in the Jenin refugee camp, home to some 14,000 Palestinians, the overwhelming majority of them civilians. The Israelis' expressed aim was to capture or kill Palestinian militants responsible for suicide bombings and other attacks that have killed more than 70 Israeli and other civilians since March 2002. The IDF military incursion into the Jenin refugee camp was carried out on an unprecedented scale compared to other military operations mounted by the IDF since the current Israeli-Palestinian conflict began in September 2000.

CHAPTER TWO

Major (Res.) Rami Kaplan

The Gaza Strip (see Maps, Figures 6, 7) has been closed off since the signing of the Oslo Accords in 1993. It holds some 1.2 million Palestinians crowded into cities, villages, and refugee camps, all within a mere 360 square kilometers. That's the size of an average U.S. city, squeezed into an eight-kilometer-wide strip of land bordered by the sea.

However, only the settlers can move about freely within the territory, so that the armed forces can maintain better control over the entire area. The Palestinians are under heavy restrictions on moving from one sealed-off location to the next, meaning that they actually live in small, disconnected communities that constitute less than 80 percent of the 360 square kilometers of the whole Gaza Strip.

In fact, 6,900 Jewish settlers control 22 percent of the land and 25 percent of the water. Eighteen settlements, along with the road leading to them, dissect the Gaza Strip, so that the Palestinians have no continuity of their own territory. Furthermore, when the settlers use the road, it is closed to Palestinians. These factors explain some of the reasons why, according to a World Bank report, 82 percent of the Palestinians in the Gaza Strip live below the poverty line on less than $2 a day. Deprived of the freedom to travel, to work, to receive medical care, to go to school, and to visit relatives, the Palestinians live in poverty surrounded by electric fences. Their very densely crowded conditions are much like prison.

The IDF's sole purpose in Gaza is to protect the settlers, patrol the border with Egypt, and enforce the closure on the Palestinians. The responsibility for enforcing these inhuman conditions has caused some soldiers to defy their orders. Rami Kaplan is one of them.

At 29, Rami looks level-headed and sharp with his short black hair and freckles. He grew up in northern Tel Aviv, a hegemonic center inhabited by the ruling bureaucratic elite, civil servants, and senior clerks. His mother, who had leftist tendencies, died when he was 13 years old. His father is a businessman who never concerned himself with the army or other political questions. Nor did his brother. Rami's inclination to excel in the framework of the army didn't come from home.

Like many Israelis, he at first saw joining the army as part of his becoming an adult. Taking on this huge new responsibility signaled his independence. Years later, however, he realized that his so-called independence meant subordination to a system that would not let him go. It dictated his values and constructed his whole frame of mind. That is why it was so hard for him to make his choice to refuse to serve in the occupied territories. Even after his refusal, he continued to think of his actions within the army's frames of reference.

A major, Rami was the highest-ranking officer to sign the objectors' letter. He was a battalion subcommander in the armored corps and did his graduate studies in political science, philosophy, and the history of ideas at Tel Aviv University. Until recently, he worked as an economics correspondent for a leading Israeli daily.

After he signed the officers' letter, Rami was expelled from his unit. Needless to say, he did not take his dismissal lightly. He continues to work as a leader out of his sense of mission and responsibility. He runs the refusers' campaign with the intensity of a military commander, advising and participating in the movement's steering committee, directing open-house meetings, and accompanying refuseniks to appointments with their commanders.

When I first met Rami Kaplan at the outset of the Courage to Refuse movement, he spoke cautiously. Afraid to trip and fall, he kept stepping over the cracks. He did not deviate from his new organization's party line.

As one of the founding members of this movement, in the early stages of the game Kaplan was willing to talk only about his military service in the occupied territories. At the time, all he wanted to do was offer testimony. For him, that meant describing the injustices that informed his choice and opening the eyes of Israeli society so it could see where it was being led.

As his refusal became more involved, Rami Kaplan became more politicized, more critical of the manifestations of the Zionist project, and more willing to take risks in voicing his protest. Yet, still cautious, he continued to declare his loyalty and sense of belonging to the nation of Israel at large. At each stage of the process, Kaplan redefined the boundaries of his criticism of the national consensus. Nevertheless, he was careful not to step outside the Israeli collective by expressing his solidarity with the Palestinians. He feared this would seem to push him into the radical left. He insisted that the Israelis first needed to see the incredible damage this occupation had done to their own nation before they could see the damage it caused the Palestinians.

Some ten weeks after the movement was launched, the IDF began a massive attack against Palestinian cities. That led the group to search for a way to amplify their protest. They convened a meeting to discuss their actions. Rami told the group that he thought the time had come to broaden their message. Even if it meant condemnation in the atmosphere of public intolerance at the time, he was willing to take the risk.

———

KAPLAN: At age 18 I found myself in the army, literally. For the next six years, the army was synonymous with my own development. It turned me from a selfish person into a serious person. I saw military service as a noble aim, as self-realization, as a moral imperative. I took it for granted that serving in the army advanced the common good.

But I hated serving in the territories and coming into contact with the civilian population. I felt that the IDF was carrying out political objectives there. I couldn't remain indifferent to the Palestinians' suffering and degraded living conditions. I didn't feel good manning a checkpoint where I'd detain or interrogate poor Palestinians heading to work at 4 in the morning.

Luckily, most of my service entailed training with tanks and preparing for full-scale war. The few times I was in the territories, my assignments were so clean they were sterile compared to the things I heard others had to do. I guess the units stationed there for longer periods have more problematic assignments. With time, they must get so callous that they also get abusive.

My last reserve duty was in Gaza. Our daily routine entailed razing areas, which, for the most part, meant uprooting orchards and fields. At first I objected, but eventually I caved in because my commander, who was also my friend, asked me to help him out. *Khisoufim*[1] is a new, sterilized Hebrew word formed to obscure the brutal destruction of community infrastructure and therefore the livelihoods of many people. These massive ground clearings look more or less like this: a tank and two or three armored bulldozers enter a fenced-off area backed by another tank. They arrive without warning to a piece of land that belongs to people who live in shacks and cinder-block houses, and

1. In Hebrew, *khisoufim* literally means "making bare," army terminology for razing an entire area of its houses, trees, and anything that may conceal a potential Palestinian ambush.

then they systematically uproot all their trees while the residents look on in dismay.

The people who live there dare not protest or even wave an angry fist at the encroaching tank. Fear forces these miserable people to stand by and watch in silence as their only source of income, fruit or olive trees sometimes 200 years old, is obliterated. They are forced to witness this unobstructed, cruel, and alien invasion of their property, their last little parcel on God's earth. Their suffering is never taken into consideration. As far as the army is concerned, they endanger the lives of Israeli soldiers and civilians.

One of these operations was in a village or a family compound. There were a few shacks and an abundant orange grove. I remember our scout hollering, "They have weapons, they have weapons!" He saw strips of cloth across their chests. In the end it turned out to be sacks for gathering fruit.

They wanted to pick as many oranges as they could before the bulldozers arrived. The ground-clearing operations were advancing toward them from day to day. When our machinery closed in on them, they began to feel afraid. Finally, they fled the grove and assembled on its edge. They watched all day while the tractors took down their trees. I sat there pulling my hair out.

During the day we'd clear entire areas by razing everything to the ground. At night we'd guard the fence to keep terrorists from getting through. We never encountered any. But every few days, a group of Palestinian laborers, looking for work in Israel, would jump it. We chased after them as if they were terrorists. We also pursued the Israeli employers who waited for them on the other side. When we'd catch the workers, they were always unarmed. After a short interrogation, the police would escort them back to Gaza.

They were just people looking for work, and we would mobilize the entire battalion as if each illegal border crossing were a terrorist operation. Since it happened at night several times a week, it exhausted us. Then one day the regiment commander assembled all the battalion commanders and said that the laborers would continue to cross the border illegally if we didn't prevent them from doing so. He handed us new firing regulations that had just been issued by the central command.

Apparently, the battalion preceding us had accidentally killed a 7-year-old boy for no reason. As we were made to understand, the new regulations had been revised because such incidents don't look good on camera. This was the only reason for the amendment. After detailing the new firing regulations, the regiment commander dictated the policy to restrict Palestinian laborers from entering Israel: "Kill them on the fence."

That was the new policy. Why on the fence? Because the regulations for opening fire are more lenient there. Once they cross that line, the regulations make it harder to shoot and kill them. The regiment commander kept repeating, "Kill them on the fence" like a mantra. The brigade commander and the battalion commander drilled it into us.

The mood in the room was such that I was afraid to stand up and protest. Were I to have pointed out that the policy was morally problematic, not to mention manifestly illegal,[2] I would have been tossed out for being a defeatist, a radical leftist, a bleeding-heart liberal who didn't

---

2. This is a term coined by Judge Benjamin Halevy following the Kufr Qassem massacre in 1956. On the day that Israel launched the Suez War against Egypt, the Israeli-Arab communities along the border with Jordan were placed under curfew. In the village of Kufr Qassem, 43 men and women and children who had not heard of the curfew returned home from working in the fields. Under army orders, they were lined up and summarily executed by members of an Israeli Border Patrol unit. In a precedent-setting decision, a court martial declared that manifestly illegal orders must not be obeyed. The members of the patrol were tried and sentenced but were soon pardoned, fined one shekel, and released. At the court martial, Judge Halevy ruled that a manifestly illegal order has a "black flag flying over it."

understand the magnitude of the task with which I'd been entrusted: an Arab-lover who lost his mind at a time of national emergency.

The regiment commander explained how we could open fire on a woman and her five children if they were walking along the fence at night. We could kill them, and later say that we identified six crouching figures advancing suspiciously. In other words, according to the firing regulations, as long as you could attribute suspicious behavior to the people you'd shot, you could do whatever you wanted in the vicinity of the fence.

When stricter regulations get handed down, the commanders grumble that they're being held back by external considerations that impair their ability to carry out operations and protect their soldiers. Commanders hate constraints, and firing regulations are a constraint.

There were leftist commanders at the briefing, and not one of them noticed that we had just received a manifestly illegal order. I didn't realize it was an illegal order, either. I just felt that the new regulations were immoral. After the briefing, I told my battalion commander what I thought about the whole thing. And when I encountered an illegal border crossing of laborers, I ordered my soldiers to shoot in the air to scare them back inside the Strip.

Netzarim is a settlement of maybe fifty Jewish families sitting smack in the middle of the Gaza Strip. There are no other settlements around it. A whole battalion reinforced by tanks and smaller forces are on hand to protect it, way more soldiers than residents. Nobody enters Netzarim by car. They only come in armored buses that sometimes transport just one child accompanied by three armored jeeps and a tank.

The settlement can only be accessed via a road that was seized for that purpose, and it effectively divides Gaza in half: north and south. The sides of this road have been cleared of the orchards, houses, and factories that used to line it for hundreds of meters in each direction.

Netzarim is a bone lodged in Gaza's throat. It's run by a small number of deranged people. Their extreme ideology of holding onto land in the middle of Palestinian territory forces Israeli society as a whole into being their accomplice.

The Eden that these people have constructed is rapidly turning into hell. Its development exploited the Palestinian population. For twenty years, this went on unhindered. Much has been written about the theft of water and the destruction of Palestinian agriculture by Mekorot[3] and the Civil Administration.[4] It's no wonder the Palestinians keep attacking this enclave by any means possible.

Crowds of Palestinian children come to the checkpoints after Friday prayers. They curse the soldiers and pelt them with stones. They try to get close, to test the limits, to taunt the almighty IDF. The soldiers shoot in the air to scare the kids. Eventually the snipers, who are more and more abundant in the territories, shoot at their legs. It's pounded into every soldier's head that the Palestinians want their children to die so they can photograph their corpses and score another point in the publicity war. If that were the case, and any reasonable person would scream that it's not, then it would only demonstrate how desperate they've become.

The extent of our fortification in Gaza is profound. And it only increases with time. We secure the roads, raze everything alongside them, and keep bringing in tanks. One day, when a mortar landed next to us inside the Green Line, people said this signaled "the next level." But it's to be expected. It's never-ending. When I saw the injustice of the situation that we're caught up in, it drove me crazy. I saw how the reservists couldn't take it, and how they swarmed the army psychiatrists in hordes. And how the regular conscripts weren't getting trained,

3. The Israeli Water Authority.
4. The Israeli body responsible for administering Palestinian civil affairs on behalf of the military government in the occupied territories, before such matters were transferred to the Palestinian Authority in areas A and B in accordance with the Oslo agreements (see Maps, Figure 3).

because they were needed in the territories. The State of Israel is shooting itself in the foot.

After all I saw in Gaza, I still didn't think about refusing to serve there, mostly because I felt responsible for my soldiers. If I weren't there with them, the chance that they would get hurt or do bad things was that much greater. After my last tour of duty in Gaza, it took me a few months to decide that I wouldn't go back anymore. I told my battalion commander, and we were about to resolve the issue quietly. We were looking for another battalion subcommander who could cover the territories while I covered everything else. Then I heard about the letter of the officers from Courage to Refuse that was being circulated.

I understood that the moral thing to do, for the state, our society, and the truth, would be to sign the letter. But I kept debating with myself. I was inclined to steer clear of the whole affair, to avoid paying the price of "coming out." I didn't want a confrontation with the army and all it would entail: ostracism, prison, and exposure. I didn't want to get sucked into the intensive political activism that signing the letter would involve, certainly not at the expense of my other commitments.

After about ten days of intensive deliberation, I heard on the radio that the IDF had bombed the Palestinian radio station in Ramallah. I signed the letter. Within a few days, I had wholly dedicated myself to the movement.

CHACHAM: When you look back and observe the changes you've gone through, how do you explain to yourself the frame of mind that directed your life for so many years?

KAPLAN: My consciousness was rather limited before and during my regular army service and much of my service in the reserves. After I was released from the army as a regular conscript, I enrolled in the university and began studying political science and business administration. I also began to read and think about the meaning of the occupation to sharpen my political positions. I noticed that Israelis lived just fine with the idea of the occupation, although if you asked them about an occupation elsewhere, like Iraq's occupation of Kuwait, they'd tell you how terrible it was. But our occupation isn't understood that way. I started to see the extent to which we view our reality through a smokescreen.

The army permeates a soldier's beliefs and thought process. Our moral judgment is systematically impaired by a variety of factors: we nurse an ideology that presents the Arab as a degenerate, conniving, dehumanized enemy; we have an unyielding commitment to the "military mission"; our military socialization exalts those who have killed and nurtures their bloodthirstiness; and we're encouraged to be part of the gang. When these factors converge in a situation of occupation, it's a disaster in the making.

In order to refuse, you must overcome a social consciousness that has been ingrained in you throughout years of education. These things take time to develop. I'm amazed at the whole process when I think of who I was during my regular service, and where I came from. Back then, I thought what I was doing was unavoidable. It takes independence to reach the opposite conclusion.

CHACHAM: Do you have a political vision?

KAPLAN: We must restore Israel's morality and core values. Israel must let the Palestinian people be, and it must enable them to establish an independent state in the territories occupied since 1967. Israel must acknowledge its role in the tragedy that has beset the Palestinian people for the past fifty years, and it must demonstrate the magnanimity to reconcile and redress these wrongs.

We must also find a creative and generous solution to the problem of the refugees without upsetting the Jewish majority. After the end of occupation, Israel must rehabilitate its relationship with all its minorities and underprivileged communities: the Arab-Israeli citizens and the weak of our society. But as long as preference is given to Jewish interests, Israel cannot treat all its citizens equally, regardless of sex, religion, ethnicity, or race. Personally, I would support a state for all its people, a state that doesn't define itself through race or nationality. But in the current circumstances the most pressing issue is that of ending the occupation.

In the Camp David negotiations, Barak ostensibly made a "generous offer" that the Palestinians refused to accept. Given that this was not the case, it's important to clarify what indeed did happen at Camp David. Barak arrived in Camp David after most members of the Knesset had lost faith in his political approach. He went there like a gambler ready to bet the whole bank: if he won, we'd get peace; if he lost, everything would go to hell.

Barak's "daring" offer to the Palestinians had clipped wings. It never included the things the Palestinians really needed, like withdrawal from the areas occupied in 1967 and a solution to the refugee problem. Barak came to the Palestinians with his offer and said, "Take it or leave it. This is all you're gonna get."

As far as the Palestinians were concerned, the offer wasn't good enough. Since their refusal threatened to bury Barak's political career, he responded in kind by painting the entire affair as their failure. He told the Israeli public that he was willing to give them everything, but the "irrational" Palestinians, confirming all the demonic notions we've ever had about them, declined at the last minute, meaning they weren't ready for real peace. This public-relations stunt was damaging precisely because it was Barak who spun it and not Sharon. It failed to save Barak, and it has proven to be a calamity as far as Israeli public opinion is concerned.

But the left's failure didn't begin with Barak. The failings of the peace camp go way back. They drew their legitimacy almost exclusively from the elite, and that's all they really cared about. Their neoliberalism advanced with the peace process at the expense of the welfare state, and that didn't offer much hope for the poor. While the rich got richer, the residents of the development towns[5] stayed as stuck as they always were.

Twenty percent of Israelis generate no income and rely on one form or another of public assistance. Everybody knows that poverty is fertile ground for nationalism and racism. The residents of the development towns, who have been neglected by the left and before that by the hegemonic socialist Mapai,[6] have become its die-hard knee-jerk opponents, and who can blame them? Many people from development towns would look at a north Tel Aviv boy like myself and feel alienated by the ideas I espouse. Especially when there are forces that incite them to reject everything I stand for.

The leftist movements in Israel, from Labor to Meretz[7] to Peace Now, never raised the flag of conscience so much as the flag of utilitarianism. The more benefits the occupation reaped, the weaker the

---

5. These towns were established between the years 1952 and 1964 in the northern periphery and the south of the country, long before the settlements in the occupied territories. New Jewish immigrants from Arab countries in Asia or Africa were settled in those towns, thus creating segregated pockets of Sephardi communities, distant from the established center populated mostly by Ashkenazi Jews. In later years, some immigrants from Ethiopia and Russia were settled in those places, but the majority of the inhabitants remain Sephardi. These towns are impoverished, neglected, and discriminated against, and they suffer from deprivation of national resources. In the last few years, as many factories here moved to Jordan and to other places where labor is cheaper, development towns suffer very high rates of unemployment.

6. A former incarnation of today's Labor party.

7. See Introduction, note 12.

objection to it. Labor is the party that occupied the territories in the first place. They're the party who kept these resources of cheap labor and free land and water in Israeli hands. There were countless opportunities to give it all back for peace with the Arabs. Labor is also the party who put the first settlements on the map, including the so-called ideological settlements of Gush Emunim.[8]

When the first Intifada erupted, the occupation became an unprofitable business for the state, and especially for those who had something to lose, the affluent sectors who make up the so-called peace camp. After the attempt to repress the uprising by "breaking the bones"[9] of the Palestinians failed, the peace camp began emphasizing the vested Israeli interest in establishing a Palestinian state and bringing about regional peace.

Speaking of French colonialism in Algeria, Albert Camus said that every act of refusal contains a "no" but also a "yes." Our letter has a negative message: "Don't serve." Already we can see that even if the number of refusers grows, the situation won't change. Our current task is to deliver a positive message and broaden the ranks. The army will manage without us.

Everything has been reduced to the question, "Is refusal permissible?" The question really is about the occupation and how we continue our efforts through our activism.

On the eve of the current Intifada, when things were still quiet, I was stationed near Qalqilya in the West Bank. We had hardly any contact with the Palestinians there. The disturbing part was the settlers. They feel that the army is subjected to political coercion and is therefore not on their side. We were supposed to evacuate an illegal encampment set up by some young Jewish extremists near Karnei Shomron.

---

8. A religious-nationalist movement that believes in the Jews' right to settle "Greater Israel."
9. A common phrase that refers to the aggressive military policy instituted by then-Minister of Defense Yitzhak Rabin.

When the time came to evacuate them, the settlers congregated by the hundreds to obstruct the operation. They blocked the road with cars and boulders and barricaded themselves in the structures, ready for a physical confrontation with the army. Opposite them stood hundreds of soldiers and policemen who were supposed to carry out the operation, and I was to lead this force.

The army gave the settlers a number of ultimatums, which they repeatedly ignored. Finally, they agreed to consult their rabbis in Jerusalem and to leave if the rabbis advised them to do so. We waited all night, sleeping next to the cars. Some of the settlers cursed us incessantly. The next day, the rabbis ordered the youth to abandon the encampment on condition that the army restore it after one month's time. And so it was. The settlers left the encampment, and the army cleared the boulders and removed the structures, only to bring them back at a later date. Gathering the forces needed to conduct this operation must have cost millions of shekels; they had to call in regular conscripts and pull police officers from other assignments.

This kind of encounter with the settlers is a common practice. The army receives orders from the political level to evacuate illegal settlements, and it has to comply. But in fact what happens on the ground is that both the army and the settlers play a game. No one seems to violate the law, but in the end the settlers get what they want under the protection of the army. As a rule, the army is not too rigid with them, though this is not always the case; in the instance I just gave you, the army was prepared to forcefully evacuate them. Yet they were promised they could return to the same place a month later. Only this time, they came back legally. How? I don't know. From what I can gather, there was nothing out of the ordinary in the army's capitulation to the settlers.

Lately, the settlers' slogans, "Let the IDF Win" and "Destroy the Palestinian Authority," are slowly winning over public opinion. The settlers, who espouse the darkest of ideologies, are leading us into an aimless war that's destroying the Zionist project. They've become so powerful that they're dragging the entire state after them in a downward spiral. We have to seize the national agenda. This country doesn't belong to them any more than it belongs to us.

There's a line in Isaiah that describes where we're at. Isaiah suggests that the people of Israel living in Judea return to a moral life, and then he warns, "If you are willing and obedient, you shall eat the good of the land; but if you refuse and rebel, you shall be devoured by the sword; for the mouth of the Lord has spoken."[10] Isaiah points to cosmic law, to the ideal, which one could also call God, in which an existence based on injustice leads to destruction, while existence based on justice leads to well-being and prosperity. This rule repeats itself throughout history. Today, in Israel, we are being devoured by the sword; we are degenerating and approaching ruination like the people of Judea, because our existence is based on injustice, first and foremost because of the occupation. Only a return to an existence based on justice can save us from this sword. Is it too late to change direction?

---

10. *Isaiah* 1:19. All biblical references in this and later chapters are taken from *The Oxford Annotated Bible*, Oxford University Press, London, 1962.

CHAPTER THREE

Lieutenant (Res.) Yaniv Iczkovitz

Yaniv Iczkovitz is a 27-year-old graduate student in the Interdisciplinary Program at Tel Aviv University. His Romanian parents immigrated to Israel in the 1960s, and he grew up among the apartment complexes and shopping centers of Rishon LeZion, a middle-class suburb of Tel Aviv. Yaniv is one of the authors of the combat soldiers' letter of refusal.

After nine years in the army, Yaniv chose to refuse his orders to serve in the occupied territories. The way he tells the story today is not how he would have told it during his service, had he told it at all. In it, two voices can be heard simultaneously: his current critical voice and the voice from his past, the one that says he still feels connected to the army, the state, and his comrades-in-arms. In his critique of the state, Yaniv does not speak like an outsider looking in; he feels part and parcel of his country.

Listening to him, I realize that he uses the concept of an ethical person following two moral codes. The first code defines the ethical person in national terms, a person who defends the right of the Jewish people to live on their land. The second code refers to people for whom human dignity and equality are paramount. In the occupation, these two codes are incompatible. This is the internal contradiction that he contends with as a part of his effort to remain within the system.

More than once in our conversation, Yaniv took his shaved head in

his hands. His revelations of injustice were accompanied by a look of cul-
pability and shame. An introvert, he spoke slowly, and he thought long
and hard between sentences, as though he were trying to sound out the
words to himself first.

Many soldiers find themselves participating in the oppression,
sensing the anguish they are causing and feeling torn inside; yet they
continue to do their job as though they were under a binding obligation
that could not be questioned. They forsake their humanity when they are
called up to serve in the name of a deeply rooted obligation to their family, society, and nation. Shouldering the burden of this obligation, they
feel it is their destiny, the commandment of a supreme authority. They
are motivated by a sense of fraternity with friends and brothers, with
whom they believe they share the ancient bond of blood. Moral questions regarding Palestinian rights appear theoretical, distant, and irrelevant in the face of these intense primordial feelings. That is the
predicament in which Yaniv found himself several months ago, before he
decided to refuse.

Like many Israelis, Yaniv had never developed social relationships
with Arabs. Despite their proximity in a small, crowded territory, the two
societies live in almost total separation. The upheaval that he described
upon learning, during his travels, that there were "smart Arabs" attests
to the way he was brought up. He came to realize that, by and large,
Israelis see Arabs through the lens of demonization, a perspective that
effectively blurs them out of existence altogether.

Yaniv described watching a Palestinian family through his binoculars. In a moment of banality, as he noticed the routine of their daily
life, he had a change of heart. Something in the texture of their life
penetrated his awareness. Their pain awakened his reason. A simple
moment of observation exposed the inhumanity of the occupation. See-

ing the Palestinian family, and giving them a place in his heart, Yaniv shattered his self-image as a confident, self-righteous Israeli officer.

———

ICZKOVITZ: You can't be moral in Gaza. It's a contradiction in terms. Can you do *khisoufim*[1] with music, perhaps with a smile? Can you give a Palestinian candy and wish him good morning after he waited for hours at a roadblock? Some say that we shouldn't refuse to serve because we could change the treatment at the checkpoints instead. We could serve them coffee and cake while they wait. What a joke.

What worries me is the people who understand that what's happening in the territories isn't right, yet they can't move beyond the idea that anything goes in the name of security. It's obvious that the Palestinians are suffering, but what can we do, given the suicide bombings? This rhetoric ignores the 35-year-long occupation, which has brought the Palestinians to a state of hopeless desperation.

I didn't grow up in a leftist home. My father is very much a hawk. He was a career officer in the army for many years. My father sits to the right of center, and my mother slightly to the left. Both of them encouraged me to enlist in an officer's track. Meanwhile, my older sister served in one of the most combative units for women. I decided to go for the most elite combat unit I could get into. Trying to get into the best unit was a game of prestige, like who has the nicest car.

From an early age I read *Air Force* magazine and *In the Camp*.[2] Maybe it sounds a little perverted, but I had a really good friend in the eighth grade, and we would read books by generals, buy plastic soldiers, and reenact military operations together. Aside from that, I played the guitar. Before my conscription, I contemplated whether to

1. See Chapter 2, note 1.
2. The IDF magazine.

go into a military band or a combat unit. In the end, I realized that I could play music after the army, and that I had a once-in-a-lifetime opportunity to serve my country.

My ambition was to become an officer. I was totally engrossed in the training. When I came home on furlough and saw civilians, they looked like they didn't know anything. In fact, a kind of chasm emerged between us, which every combat soldier can attest to, between those who were there and those who weren't there and so had no idea. It gave us a sense of superiority, I'm sorry to say.

You want me to tell you about events I experienced in the army? Eight months after I enlisted, we were in Jenin and Qabatia in the West Bank. I remember patrolling in a jeep in Qabatia at the height of the peace process. This was my first real encounter with the Palestinian population. I saw Palestinian children swimming in garbage, literally. They would dive into dumpsters in search of food. My commander forbade us to throw food to them. I disobeyed that order. I threw all the combat meals we had in our post to those kids. That was the first time I disobeyed an order. I even wrote a poem about it. I was in shock. Starving Palestinian children diving into garbage dumpsters! If someone saw Jewish children doing that in Tel Aviv, the entire state would be up in arms.

The second thing I remember is conducting arrests for the General Security Services, the GSS.[3] You'd walk through the alleys of Qabatia at 3 A.M., petrified that they'd throw a cinder block down from a roof onto you. You'd have no idea what you were doing, why you were doing it, whom you were going to meet, or what the context was for the operation. They'd say, "Take this map. This is the house. Go there. Your job is to enter the house with your commander and conduct a search." At that time, I had been in the army for only eight months. You wouldn't even know what you were looking for. They'd say, "Arms." You were operating in a fog.

---

3. Also commonly referred to as the Shabak.

We entered a Palestinian home. The entire family was sleeping in the living room. The woman of the house opened the door. We didn't break in violently. I searched the house and opened the closets. All the while, scenarios from Hollywood movies ran through my mind, that someone would jump out from one of the closets. Then my flashlight went out. The family handed me a lantern. When I took it, it fell and shattered on the floor. My commander told me to pick up the broken pieces. I collected them all. At that moment I was furious with him. We're in the middle of an operation here, I thought to myself. Why should I take a broom and clean up? It didn't fit with the movie. Imagine a Hollywood film where the army enters a house, and one of the soldiers stands there with a broom sweeping the floor. I was really pissed off. If you're in a military operation, you break things. In the end, I concluded that it was a very humane thing to do, even though I never understood what we were doing there in the first place.

The third incident was the worst. A stone landed in a jeep and a soldier got hurt. Every time the patrol jeep would pass an olive grove, it would be pelted with stones. So we decided to ambush them. I didn't participate in the ambush, but my friends told me about it. They caught two 14-year-old stone-throwers. One of them managed to escape, and the other one didn't.

My platoon commander, my company subcommander, another officer, and nine soldiers were there. They told me how they beat the kid senseless. Which is okay, maybe, because he threw a stone, and "the one who comes to kill us, we shall arise early to kill him." But what's not okay is that they continued to beat him after he was bound. The platoon commander hit him with a rifle until the rifle broke. In other words, the beating was brutal. This child went to the hospital in critical condition with shattered ribs.

The army has become both the executive branch and the judicial branch. They not only caught him, they also decided what punishment he deserved. What bothered me the most was the investigation that followed. The unit commander decided that they had used reasonable force. I understood then that there had been a terrible cover-up. There is no understanding of the roles of the army, the law, and human rights. Okay, you caught him in an ambush and handcuffed him, so take him to court.

CHACHAM: How did you keep going?

ICZKOVITZ: I'll tell you the truth. I didn't think about what I was doing, or why, or in what historical context. When I felt overwhelmed, I'd express my feelings in a poem, or I'd fight with my girlfriend. I'd explode emotionally. The question of the territories was never a moral one. We were taught that the 1967 war started as a war against us. What should we do if someone fights us and wants to kill us? The Palestinian population never struck me as an entity that warranted serious consideration.

The other thing that influenced me was a school trip to Poland. In Poland, I felt the humiliation of the Jews, and I said, "Never again!" We need a strong army. In retrospect, I understand that this was precisely what these trips were meant to accomplish. That's exactly why they took us there.

I always had the feeling that if it were not for the state, I would not exist. Therefore, a war for the survival of the Jewish people couldn't possibly be immoral. We didn't set out to be an occupier, but rather to defend ourselves. I felt that settling ourselves on the land[4] was legiti-

4. The assumption held by most of the refuseniks and most Israelis is that Jewish dwellings within the borders internationally agreed upon in 1948 are legitimate. However, most see settlements outside of the Green Line, in those territories occupied after the 1967 war, as illegitimate. Different words in Hebrew are used to describe settlements. The Jewish settlements established in pre-1948 Palestine are now called *hityashvut* (settlement, colony). After 1967, the new colonies in the occupied territories were called *hitnakhalut*, a different word with the same meaning. In May 2002, the Director General of the Israeli Broadcast Authority banned the use of *hitnakhalut* from the Israeli airwaves altogether. Now the word *hityashvut* is again used for Jewish settlements in the territories, to lend legitimacy to the stigmatized settlers of today.

mate. Everything that the state has done is morally justified and neces-sary because of the Holocaust. These are the ideas I absorbed not only at home but in school, in history class, from the media, all around me.

My belief in all these truisms eroded shortly before the Israeli withdrawal from Lebanon. For four years, it was my duty to risk my life to protect Israeli villages and towns on the northern border. I was an officer in Lebanon. I knew that the Hezbollah[5] were terrorists, and that we had to kill terrorists. But I never asked why we were in the secu-rity zone. At first I was very angry with the Four Mothers movement[6] because, as an officer, I lost a lot of soldiers in Lebanon. I couldn't accept the contention that we were there for no reason. What about the towns and villages of the northern Galilee? Why should we forsake them? Ever since I became a soldier, from day one, I was told that my principal aim was to kill terrorists in Lebanon. The greatest prestige in the IDF was to produce the dead body of a terrorist. That's what you were created for. That's why you were given a beret.

They really scare you with Hezbollah. They tell you that if you withdraw to the border, Hezbollah will try to take Jerusalem. They tell us today that if we leave the territories, the Palestinians will try to take Tel Aviv. These claims, as absurd as they may sound, resonated with me back then. Fear always works. The Hezbollah are presented as Mus-lim fanatics whose only purpose in life is to annihilate you. After my release, I began researching the history of Hezbollah. It turns out they're not trying to conquer Tel Aviv, and not even Kiryat Shmona,

5. Formed in 1982 in response to the Israeli invasion of Lebanon, this Lebanon-based radical Shi'a group takes its ideological inspiration from the Iranian revolution and the teachings of the Ayatollah Khomeini. The group's governing body is led by Secretary General Hassan Nas-rallah. Hezbollah formally advocates the ultimate establishment of Islamic rule in Lebanon and the liberation of all occupied Arab lands, in which they include Jerusalem. Although close-ly allied with and often directed by Iran, the group may have conducted operations that were not approved by Tehran. While Hezbollah does not share the Syrian regime's secular orien-tation, the group has been a strong tactical ally in helping Syria advance its political objectives in the region.

6. See Chapter 1, note 1.

a town at the northern border of Israel and Lebanon, which suffered heavy retaliation from the Hezbollah.

When members of the security establishment began to voice their criticism, and when our soldiers started to drop like flies, something shifted in my head. I began volunteering for the Four Mothers movement and lecturing in schools. Then we withdrew, and I saw that if we just determined the borders, things would work out. I understood that our entire sojourn in Lebanon had been pointless. It strikes me now that a crime has gone unpunished. One of the tasks of the refuseniks should be to insist on redressing it.

Nonetheless, I continued to serve. When they broke the Arabs' bones in the first Intifada,[7] it seemed totally legitimate to me. I never knew they had rights to this land. Only with the Oslo Accords did I come to understand that the Arabs have a case. When the Oslo process began, I thought it was excellent. Finally, they would have a state, and we would live in peace. To me, Rabin represented a virtuous Israel— not because he became a pacifist, but because he understood that you can't defeat people who want freedom and that we had to make a compromise. I finally understood that if things improved for them, things would improve for us as well.

CHACHAM: How can you account for the gap between what you know now and what you were oblivious to before?

ICZKOVITZ: It was only after asking myself whether it was necessary to occupy people's territory that I began reading the history of the Palestinian conflict. Most of these studies were at Oxford. I studied for two semesters in England, and that's where I first met Palestinians and Arabs. I didn't make friends with them. On the contrary, we had a few arguments. But I heard them. When you hear an entirely different ver-

7. See Chapter 2, note 9.

sion of the story, you understand that you have the Zionist perspective just as they have the Palestinian perspective. That influenced me greatly. I also understood that the image of the Arab as we see it is a cultural construct.

When you're a kid, the Arab is the person you must avoid at all costs. We had Arabs who swept the staircases in our building, and my mother was afraid to let us go out whenever they were around. The Arab throws stones and Molotov cocktails in the Intifadas. And in the history we were taught, the Arab is the one who wants to kill you. It takes a while to figure out that the Arab is a human being with a history. At Oxford I finally understood this, not just intellectually but also emotionally. When you read Edward Said, for example, who is a Palestinian Arab, you understand that they can also be intelligent.

This was a total transformation of my consciousness. There's nothing more difficult than breaking cultural constructs that have been embedded in you since you were born. There's nothing harder, nothing more complex than that. It requires immense psychological and philosophical effort. Look at the Americans; they're no different from us. They, too, dehumanize the Arabs, whom they see as the epitome of the Other, from Hollywood movies to what's happening now in Afghanistan and Iraq.

This attitude enables Jewish Israelis to discriminate against Arab-Israeli citizens. And not only them. Religious and Sephardic Jews are not first-class citizens in Israel, either. The secular Ashkenazi Jews serve in the elite combat units that define the essence of the Israeli. If you're not white, and if you listen to Um Kulthum[8] and play with a masbaha,[9] you are more like an Arab than you are an Israeli.

Barak committed a historical crime when he demonized Arafat after the failure at Camp David. It was Barak's fault as much as

8. Legendary Egyptian singer.
9. A string of 33 beads designating the 99 names of Allah in Islam, commonly used by Arab Muslims, Christians, and Jews alike.

Arafat's. With his about-face, Barak created a consensus that's very difficult to break today. He took the position that Arafat was a liar, and that therefore there was no interlocutor in the territories. This discourse is now shared by the left and the right. He said that if we wanted to return the territories, there would be no one to return them to. This is an absurd contention, and yet the left fell for national unity in Sharon's government and became a branch of the right.

The Labor party is coming apart, and Meretz, the Israeli social democratic peace party, can be neither seen nor heard. Yossi Sarid[10] is a hawk who objected to the withdrawal from Lebanon. The chairman of the opposition is the chairman of silence. The biggest mistake of the left is its preoccupation with security issues. They have ignored crucial social sectors that today they can no longer reach. Today, when the left speaks, these groups plug their ears. It's a sin that began with the establishment of the state, and I doubt it can be undone.

CHACHAM: Tell me about the steps that led to your refusal.

ICZKOVITZ: Three months ago, I was in Gaza, and I did what I did. When I came home, I felt as though I had a split personality. In my civilian life, I never harm anybody. I even try to be kind. I'm basically a good, moral guy. I don't go around at night robbing old ladies. I understood that I wasn't going back to the territories ever again. I talked it over with a friend who shared my feelings. We concluded that we couldn't just refuse our orders and sit at home. We're Zionists and patriots, and we have a responsibility toward our soldiers. Our refusal might be a very righteous act, but it won't bring about results beyond the individual level. That's why we initiated the refuseniks' letter.

The same sense of commitment and responsibility that led us to become combat officers informed our decision to make sure our sol-

10. Leader of Meretz.

diers didn't think we were abandoning them. We wanted them to realize that we were struggling for them as well. Most of them didn't want to be there, either. We wanted to tell them that in a democratic state, it can be one's duty to refuse orders!

A lot of people ask us, "Why do this now? This hurts state security." After we finally leave the territories, a lot of people will have to account for why they did what they're doing now. What we're doing in the territories is an offense for generations to come. As of yet, we can't estimate how terrible it is. When the Palestinians write the history of the first and second Intifadas, and obviously they too have their own shit to deal with like suicide bombings, the truth about what the IDF did will come out, and it's going to be horrifying.

After refusing my orders, I was thrown out of my unit. This is not army policy. The decision is up to the commanders. Usually they prefer to settle the matter quietly and if possible without media attention. That was the army policy toward territories refusers for years. Only a few were sent to prison. My relations with the soldiers who, until recently, were under my command are still strong. They are the people with whom I've served since we were regular conscripts. We've always done reserve duty together. Some of them are my best friends. They know everything about me, the way brothers do. My refusal caused some unpleasantness, but the ties weren't severed.

Most combat units are made up of basically ethical people. They're not blameworthy. They don't do what they do out of malice. It's blindness. There's a contradiction between who you are and what you do there. The question is whether you're willing to accept the fact that there's a contradiction, and whether you're willing to resolve it. If it's more important to you to follow orders, because you believe it's necessary, then your problem is solved. But if you're unwilling to accept things as they are, and you start to wonder if it's all really necessary, then you're asking questions. It's easier to be on the side of the one who does not ask questions, in the heart of the consensus, where you're regarded as an ethical person anyway.

We are the IDF! We're the children of the mainstream who are breaking their consensus. It's not out of fear, it's not because we're spoiled, it's because we have caused a terrible injustice to an entire people. We're breaking the rules because we have no other choice. We have an obligation to refuse. It's an historical role we must play. It's the most important thing we can do. It's the only alternative to what's happening over there.

Regarding your question, at what moment did I decide to refuse. . . . Strangely enough, it happened at a very mundane moment. A few months ago, I did reserve duty. When you're in the field, there are three things that you usually do. Either you perform guard duty, observing the Palestinian population through binoculars, or you stand inside a pillbox, a checkpoint lookout, and prevent Palestinians from moving while allowing free passage to Jews—in other words, you're implementing explicitly racist policies. Or you patrol homes, orchards, and greenhouses. One day in the pillbox, for no apparent reason, I observed a Palestinian family through my binoculars. They lived near the post. I saw how they woke up in the morning and dressed the children, how the children went to school, and how the grandparents went to work in the greenhouses. They lived in a pitiful shack with a tin roof. At lunch, they rested and smoked nargila.[11] Then the children returned from school and helped the adults with the farming. I watched them through my binoculars for six hours. I saw every detail of their daily lives, and it pained me.

11. A water pipe.

CHAPTER FOUR

Staff Sergeant (Res.) Tal Belo

A SHORT STORY

That night I was a little drunk. We were sitting around drinking in honor of Daniel. He emigrated from France so he could faithfully serve the country and the army and be with his girlfriend, Tali, a military social worker. We opened a bottle of Johnnie Walker that Tali's brother gave her and we were listening to the Doors and smoking some hash. You can't be a real Nahal[1] soldier without drinking Johnnie Walker, listening to the Doors, or smoking hash. And the select few partake in all three. We'd just gotten back from Lebanon, and after a week of R & R we were sent straight to the territories, to Gaza.

There's no place like Gaza, with its blue sea and excellent hummus. Including a ton of pita, cracked olives, and french fries, it won't cost you more than ten shekels. Hell, you'll even get change back.

Let me tell you about the olives from Gaza. First of all, they're the bitterest olives in the world. Gazans say that the olives get their bitterness from life in the Gaza Strip, from the strain of the occupation, and the one before, and then the one before that. Their saltiness will drive you crazy, too. That comes from the tears of the Gazan women. The tears they shed in the groves seep into the olives themselves.

---

1. Nahal is the Hebrew acronym for *Noar Halutzi Lohem*, Fighting Pioneer Youth. It is a military cadre combining military service in a combat unit with civilian service in a newly founded kibbutz or moshav (a collective or semi-collective agricultural settlement).

The women of Gaza are the true heroes. While the men tend to the miseries of life, looking for ways to liberate themselves from this or that occupation, the women take care of the kids, prepare the food, and work in the groves. In the groves all alone, they'll cry for their youth, for their dreams, and for their sons who were killed or imprisoned or will be soon.

The olives absorbed all of it. Contrary to general opinion, it made them taste great and they went well with whiskey. Suddenly I thought about my mother, who wasn't sleeping at night. When I tried to explain to her that all we did was drink whiskey and eat cracked olives, she didn't believe me. She started to cry and said she was scared. That she had bad dreams. Mom and her dreams. I told her not to worry and not to cry. I said that if she kept on, the water in the Israeli aquifer was going to get salty and it would be her fault. That's what had happened in Gaza. It didn't help, though. There's no one like Mom.

Tali said that Jim Morrison was king and started dancing. She was so beautiful, that Tali! Her direct manner, her flat stomach, her breasts and her nipples that stood up like two little hills on a prairie. When Daniel joined her, they kissed. I sat there by myself and thought about how Daniel was a victim. His life got screwed up, and no one had paid any attention.

Last week, during a demonstration near the Green Mosque, Daniel accidentally fired some shots into the crowd. A pregnant woman from Gaza was hit. I ran to help, but she was already dying. She gave me a sad look with tears in her eyes. She looked like she was in her fifth month, and I knew she had lost her baby since she was bleeding heavily from the abdomen. It took me awhile to insert the IV and start her transfusion. Then she died at 6 P.M.

Roni, the doctor, and I began to cry. Manny, the driver, mumbled that she was just an Arab, and so what if she died? But I could see he was having a hard time with it. I kissed him on his forehead and told him to drive back to headquarters. No one said a word to Daniel.

There was an investigation, and they decided that the whole thing had been an accident. A stray bullet. But no one talked to Daniel anymore.

I told Roni that Daniel needed some time off, that we needed to talk to him, that he seemed disturbed. But Roni was busy, and we were all busy. There were more demonstrations, and then more people got killed. I felt like I was slowly going crazy.

They taught us to fire our rifles, prepare ambushes, jump from airplanes, carry our gear, run, hit the ground, get up and run again. They forgot to teach us to talk, cry, and forgive ourselves.

Daniel looked at Tali, gave her another kiss, and said that he was stepping out for a second to take a leak. I asked him if he wanted some company. Nah, he said, stay here and keep an eye on Tali for me. So I stayed with Tali.

A minute later, we heard a shot.

Tal Belo
1992

Tal Belo is a tall man, with brown hair and a kind of robust masculinity. He grew up in Ramat Gan, a comfortable middle-class neighborhood where many of the residents are Holocaust survivors. His mother was born in Iraq and his father in Turkey. His parents, both Labor party supporters, came to Israel at a young age. His father worked for the Elite food factory and brought home a lot of chocolate. His mother is a housewife. At 29, Tal lives in Bat Hefer, a new community in the vicinity of Natanya.

There, beautiful houses sit behind a tall, thick security wall that follows the Green Line on the border of the Palestinian city of Tulkarm. He lives with his wife and two young children. His Sephardi background is important to him, but he would rather define himself as an Israeli. He outlines his Israeli identity in his own terms, and he determines his own moderate, middle-of-the-road attitude. His individualism manifests itself in his practice of alternative Chinese medicine; in the army, he serves as a medic. This is one family man who likes to get away and find himself in the desert.

Tal says he feels connected to the land. He loves its light, its smells, its people, all of its people, and even the sweat produced by its heat. He hates extreme positions that alienate others. Though he has deep reservations about militancy, he is anything but a rebel. Careful not to put himself in a position in which his humanism contradicts his loyalties, he directs his loyalties toward the immediate sphere of his relationships, his own family, and particularly his parents, who took great pains not to expose him to the trauma of their displacement as immigrants.

Tal sees the occupiers as victims alongside the occupied. This approach is evident in his Gaza story, in which the killer is also a victim. While one might argue with this point of view, he expresses a level of

compassion that you would be hard pressed to find among most Israeli soldiers, who generally display total indifference to the plight of Palestinian civilians.

CHACHAM: In what way does your story convey how you perceive yourself as a soldier in the occupied territories?

BELO: We are weak because we aren't fighting for our homes. My story about Gaza shows it. Otherwise Daniel wouldn't have killed himself. When a soldier believes in what he's doing, he can contend with anything. He'll say, "It's either you or me." But that's not the case in the territories. We don't have the same enthusiasm that my father did during the Six Day War or the Yom Kippur War. I know because I've read his letters. I couldn't write letters like that.

CHACHAM: Say more about your parents.

BELO: They're conformists. They always say, "Think what you want, but go with the flow." That's how I was raised. My background is a little mixed up. I didn't grow up with a Sephardic consciousness.[2] My identity is Israeli. I'm aware of my parents' background, but they raised me to be Israeli.

CHACHAM: When you say that you didn't grow up with a Sephardic awareness, what do you mean?

---

2. Israeli society is ethnically divided between Jews of European descent and Jews from Arab countries. The latter are called Sephardim or Mizrahim. The European Jews, Ashkenazim, although not the majority, are socioeconomically predominant.

BELO: As a kid I played the piano and didn't learn to play the oud.[3] I regret that, so I intend to teach my kids to speak Arabic and play the oud. That's important to me in a political sense.

I had a mainstream childhood. I was in a left-wing Zionist youth movement. I enlisted in the Nahal. During my compulsory service, I also facilitated Jewish-Arab youth groups.[4] Through these programs, I made friends with Palestinians from Laqiya, Ramallah, and Beit Jala. My connections with them continue to this day. Now that the situation in the territories is so bad, we talk on the phone all the time.

CHACHAM: What did your parents say about your refusal?

BELO: My parents don't approve of my refusal, but our home is an open environment. There are four of us siblings, and each of us is free to do whatever he or she wants without fear of condemnation. My mother doesn't hate Arabs. She wants peace. In her eyes, the Arabs are not evil maniacs out to destroy us. Her perspective is similar to that of German Jews who don't think that all Germans are Nazis or that the German language should be banned from the home. What she cares about is not justice, but peace. And that her daughter should become a doctor—simple things. She is a believer. My entire family is religiously observant.

In fact, I don't feel completely at ease with my refusal. I think of my father, who wouldn't refuse. I don't like the idea of going against his wishes, because he's a courteous, sensitive, and modest man who wouldn't hurt anyone intentionally. I also feel uncomfortable vis-à-vis the parents of a friend of mine who was killed in the territories. I'm afraid to face them. I also don't like the immodest tone of the refuseniks' letter, though I realize that the movement might not have

3. Arabic lute.

4. There are some youth movements that work toward friendly coexistence between Arabs and Jews. They bring together boys and girls from both communities to spend time together and share discussions.

gotten off the ground without a sense of urgency and a hint of mega-lomania. But I hope that when a permanent settlement begins to be negotiated, the movement will disband quietly.

Just because not everyone refuses doesn't mean they don't agree with us. It's hard to go against the grain. I understand that. I'm no better than they are. Nor am I any better than the settlers. If someone offered them a practical solution, they would consider it. Not all of the settlers want to embitter the lives of Arabs.

If you want to be persuasive, you need to send a message of compassion. I don't agree that we're fighting "a war for peace in the settlements."[5] The settlements must be evacuated, but we should remember that we aren't there just because of the settlements. The chief of staff claims that we're there for security reasons. The Orthodox claim is that we're there because of the Jewish holy sites. Compassion for all people involved, including the settlers, motivates my refusal. Their evacuation will be traumatic, and we need to plan ahead to meet their needs. In the long run, the settlers' lives will change for the better, though.

I also have a hard time with the fact that I have friends who chose to stay in the army instead of refusing. It creates a dilemma for me. I have a draft order next month. And I know that if I don't go with my company, they won't have a medic. Some of the guys are angry with me. They insist that they don't commit war crimes. Incidentally, that's why you can't convince people with such an assertion.

If you're there, you're committing crimes whether you like it or not. I'm no pacifist, and I wouldn't mind serving in the territories if the army could avoid committing war crimes, but they can't. That's impossible. Officers and soldiers don't want to harm civilians intentionally. But when an ambulance drives up, you don't know if there's a terrorist or a pregnant woman in it. Both sides dread this kind of contact.

5. A slogan advanced by the refuseniks that cites the official Israeli name for the 1982 invasion of Lebanon, the "War for Peace in the Galilee." By invoking this name, the refuseniks are suggesting that the current war is also of dubious intent.

I've been doing reserve duty for the past seven years. The last two times I managed to avoid serving in the territories by doing other jobs. I also did whatever I could to avoid going to prison. I could have continued to find ways around serving in the territories by producing false medical exemptions, for example. But I decided to refuse instead. If it were only Arabs who were getting hurt, maybe I wouldn't have said, "No more!" But I'm not as righteous as I'd like to be. I was motivated in part by the fact that the present reality is hurting me too.

I'm not political. I speak from personal experience when I say I can't stand it anymore. For the past few years, I've felt ashamed of what's going on. Only someone who has been there can understand. How do you explain to yourself that 100 meters from here, there are people living in the depths of hell? I hear people say, "What can we do? Their leaders brought it upon them, it's not our responsibility! We're a peace-loving people. We gave them everything. They didn't want it. Their leaders don't want peace, so let them rot in hell." Even disillusioned leftists say these things. That's the general sentiment these days.

I heard the minister of defense say, "We will kill them one by one with F16s. If the fighter jets cause collateral damage, too bad! There's nothing we can do about it." Hearing this, I cringe. We're becoming wicked. If our leaders did something so that soldiers wouldn't die, and gunships wouldn't bomb Palestinian towns, and Palestinians didn't have an excuse to blow themselves up in our cities, I wouldn't have to refuse.

As for specific experiences that pushed me to refuse, I remember a massive rally during the first Intifada.[6] Thousands of marchers from Hamas and Fatah were carrying olive branches, while we watched them miserably from our jeep. It looked like a movie. Finally, the last

6. It is important to note that the first Intifada, especially in its initial stages, was not armed. Only after its suppression did violence escalate.

protesters marched past us and said, "If you don't give us peace, we'll get you good!" They sounded like the rival gang in the neighborhood. You don't understand what's going on there. The feeling is that nobody really gets it. Sometimes we'd play football with them. We even reached an agreement with the residents of one building, where we had set up a lookout, that we'd keep the noise down during their siesta.

You see how everybody plays their part: the brigadier general, the soldier, the settler, the Palestinian civilian. It's like a game where the so-called good guys are after the so-called bad guys who throw stones at us and make provocations. All of us are just caught up in the game. After you play the game for too long, you don't know who you are anymore, and you believe in the makeshift roles. If I weren't playing the game, I would never have ordered a 40-year-old man to climb an electric pole just to remove a PLO flag.

I remember how I detained him. He was a man with a mustache, holding a black leather briefcase. I cocked my rifle and ordered him to climb the pole. On the third attempt, he managed to get the flag down. Today I'm sure his son is a suicide bomber, or at least a potential one, thanks to me. We did this all the time. We didn't just abuse one boy's father. It was a regular assignment for us in the first Intifada. The PLO was the enemy, not a partner in dialogue.

It's crazy. Think about the stakes: flags, not life and death. Not "the one who comes to kill you, arise early to kill him," just flags. That was the routine. Palestinians would hang flags, and we'd detain passersby and insist that they remove them. In retrospect, it's hard for me to believe how blind I was. I'll be terribly disappointed if my children do the things I did.

People here don't understand what it means to have your orchard uprooted, to be arrested without trial, or to be told, "I'm killing you because I've decided you're dangerous, even if you're the wrong guy, because there happens to be another guy in your village with the same name." What will you tell him afterward, "Sorry it happened"?

There's a Chinese proverb that says those who have eaten cannot understand those who are hungry. The Israeli public thinks that the people in the territories are programmed to hate us. It's not like that. The reality is far more complex than that. It's not that they want their children to commit suicide; it's that they live in such misery they have nothing to lose. We've been indoctrinated that the Arabs hate us, and that's a manipulative distortion that serves the interests of the army and the politicians, whether Labor or Likud.[7]

After Goldstein's massacre in the Tomb of the Patriarchs,[8] I saw all the blood and the bodies, heard the screams, and felt the horror in that beautiful and sacred place. I couldn't possibly describe it. It was on the eve of Purim.[9] The next day I arrived at the brigade's headquarters and everyone, right-wingers and left-wingers, was still in shock. We stood around as Hanan Porat[10] gave a TV interview. He said, "First of all, I want to wish the people of Israel a happy holiday!" I heard him and thought, Doesn't he understand that it's not a happy holiday, because a tragedy has happened, and it's not just the Arabs' tragedy? The other soldiers felt the same. We were all heartbroken.

I'll tell you about another disturbing incident. A friend of mine was serving in the Duvdevan[11] unit. One day he called to tell me how they had ransacked a house. He found brand-new sneakers in his size,

7. The right-wing national Likud is one of Israel's major conservative parties, formed in preparation for the 1973 elections.

8. On February 25, 1994, a Jewish settler named Baruch Goldstein sprayed automatic gunfire on worshipers praying in a mosque in the Tomb of the Patriarchs, a holy site in Hebron for both Islam and Judaism, killing 29 Muslims before he himself was killed.

9. A festive Jewish holiday.

10. A leader of the settler movement and a member of the Knesset from the extreme right-wing Tehiya party.

11. See Chapter 1, note 5.

and he took them. Apparently, it happens a lot in his unit. He came home and showed them to his mother. She said, "Why on earth would you wear an Arab's shoes?" She was disturbed that they had belonged to an Arab. She didn't say, "Why did you take them? Give them back!"

I know this guy. He would never think to steal anything from anyone. But the occupation gives him license to do just about anything. You allow yourself to beat Arabs. I did it too. You don't realize that you degenerate in these situations, and all of a sudden you're stuck with sneakers or a camera that you have no idea what to do with.

CHACHAM: What's so striking about your Gaza story is your strong feeling for the place. It's not a common attitude among Israeli soldiers, who rarely look at the territories they're sent to with such an open heart and mind.

BELO: Gaza is part of my personal experience. For the same reason that Hebron, the Tomb of the Patriarchs, is, and Bethlehem: all of them are. You can build a physical border, but not a spiritual one. The reason I'm still living here, instead of in Australia or New Zealand, is my longing for these places and for being there with them. I am kind of an Arab!

I was born in this place. Every year, I experience the same salty heat waves they do. My entire history, the small history of my family and the big history of this place, is here. When I'm in Jerusalem, I imagine the Temple. When I'm in Hebron, I imagine Abraham with some camels.

CHACHAM: But remember that Abraham is also Ishmael's father.

BELO: Yes, but in our story he sent Ishmael packing.

CHACHAM: That's the story that we always tell; one story takes the place of the other. Muslims tell it differently.

BELO: There isn't one truth hanging over all of them. It all depends on who's telling the story. The one who tells the story determines the truth.

CHACHAM: The settlers believe that theirs is the one and only truth, and that Abraham bequeathed the land to them. How are you different from them?

BELO: On the material level. I don't need these places to belong to me exclusively. I'm satisfied just by being able to go there. I understand the longing, but I don't understand the need to possess.

CHACHAM: So it's a matter of control?

BELO: I think so. There's no need to rule. When I served in Gaza I would finish my duties, go shower, and sit looking out at the sea. It's the calmest stretch of sea in the country. Gaza is a beautiful place. It's magical. When you see the world through the bitter olives and the blue sea, you just want to survive. I'm just looking for ways to survive. I'm not asking for much out of life: to drink espresso, to barbecue, to get drunk, to read, to dance, the small pleasures.

I believe that we need to live with the Arabs. Oslo was supposed to be about living next to them but not seeing them anymore. The Oslo plan was to divide the land. They're over there in their own state, and we're here in ours. You can't put up electric fences between us. The people who suggest that we do so are the same people who still demonize the Arabs. That's nonsense! Our dream is to live in this area. If we don't learn to get along with the Arabs, we won't be able to live here. We'll continue to live in constant fear. We live among Arab states that have their own distinctive language, culture, music, and traditions. It's not as if we're living in Europe or America, where your neighbors are the same. Our fear of the Arab is our fear of the Other. The idea that they'll destroy us is misguided. There's no absolute evil, and even if there were, the Arabs wouldn't have a monopoly over it.

As for your question about whether I would still live here if the state were no longer defined as the state of the Jewish people, but rather the state of all its citizens, in an enlightened world, yes I would. But in today's world, it's unrealistic. There's too much tension and trepidation. In the future, though, there's no other choice for our survival, as opposed to our domination.

I look at people as a medic, and I do so not only when they're injured. It's my job to look people over, and to do so with empathy. Doing this without empathy is dangerous. When you see a fellow soldier get shot, or when you see someone explode, or when you talk to a settler who believes that the Tomb of the Patriarchs is the holiest site on earth, you feel compassion. It's not hard.

When does it become difficult? When you divide the world into two sides: I'm like this and he's like that. The Western world is structured this way. It's cold and cruel, and it requires you to be the same. If you come along with a middle-of-the-road message, or an expression of understanding, it's seen as ambiguous.

Both sides are victims, and I don't want to start measuring who is worse off.

CHAPTER FIVE

Lieutenant (Res.) Guy Grossman

Guy Grossman is a 29-year-old reserve officer in the artillery corps and a graduate student in philosophy at Tel Aviv University. He hails from Raanana, an affluent town in the heart of Israel characterized by small well-tended houses surrounded by greenery. His mother was born in Australia and his father in England.

His mother is not convinced that refusing his orders is the right thing to do, but she is nonetheless proud of her son for fighting for what he believes in, especially if it means turning Israel into a better place to live. His younger brother, a paratrooper, is not sure that he will sign the refuseniks' letter. He agrees that the occupation is awful, but he does not agree with the call for total refusal. As for most of Guy's friends, they are leftists, but not all of them embrace his position either.

Guy Grossman has been attending Peace Now demonstrations since he was 15 years old. When he was 16, he spray-painted the slogan "The Occupation Corrupts!" across the city. At 18, he enlisted in an elite combat unit and did not see any contradiction between these two positions. As a soldier, he voted for Meretz.[1] In other words, he voted for withdrawal from the territories, but he continued to serve the occupation with his body.

This contradiction is typical of most, if not all, Meretz voters and leaders. Meretz joined the ruling Labor coalition in the 1990s and, in so

1. See Introduction, note 12.

doing, accepted the continued expansion of settlements after the signing of the Oslo Accords. Somehow, the belief that the occupation was nearing its end justified the policies that were carried out in the interim. Whether consciously or unconsciously, a vote for Meretz became a de facto vote for prolonged occupation.

The Israeli sense of self that Grossman describes is common. The self is tied to the state as if by an umbilical cord: state and self are one. Only great distances sever that tie. From afar, one can develop an autonomous "I" that looks critically at the state and one's public identity. The construction of a distinct, discerning personal voice that challenges the ethos of total devotion to the state does not occur all at once. It is a protracted process. Oftentimes travel abroad breaks down the moral base that sustains such a symbiotic relationship between culture and identity. As soon as the moral-national-ideological base collapses, attests Grossman, we see our total indifference to the injustices of occupation for the first time.

Like many others, he describes a moment when he realized that he had been lied to, and this was the turning point that led him to refuse. The extent to which he felt disillusioned reflects his prior confidence in the military and the magnitude of its unquestionable authority. Once the lie was uncovered, it served as his point of no return. There were a few instances, and Grossman describes one of them, when the IDF spokesperson's claims were eventually revealed to be fallacious, as he tried to cover things up in order to make the army look more humane.

Grossman's testimony from Hebron demonstrates how the occupation functions, how it perpetuates a daily routine of brutality against the occupied civilian population. The eye cannot see and the ear cannot hear those defined as the enemy.

—

GROSSMAN: I served in the army for four years, first as a regular con-script and then briefly as a career officer in a combat unit. Calling myself Lieutenant Grossman was a big part of my identity. In time, I understood that that was not all of who I am. But back then, I could-n't differentiate between my social status and my own sense of self, between enlisting in an elite unit to protect the state and the construc-tion of my own identity.

Today I'm critical of our presence in the territories, but back then I had no qualms about being a soldier. I didn't have a well-formed civil-ian sense of myself. I gave the state too much credit. Only after I was released from the army and became a civilian again did I conceive of myself first as a civilian and then as a soldier. Only then did I begin to think along new lines. In retrospect, my transformation began when I went abroad. I was released from duty in 1994, and I left immediately for a one-year trip to Central and South America by myself. That's where it started. The further you get from your state, your home, and your friends, the closer you get to yourself.

Even after my conscience started bothering me, I continued to serve in the territories. The conscience is flexible. It reacts to temporal and environmental influences. With the peace process in the making, I thought I needed to be there in order to help it progress in an orderly fashion. In 1995, I didn't know the things that I know today. I naively thought that Rabin and Arafat had already discussed the stumbling blocks and made the hard decisions, but they just weren't telling us about it yet. That they were working on softening the hearts and minds of the two publics. When they said "Gaza and Jericho first," I thought they meant much more. Everybody believed in Oslo, right?

Throughout my military service, refusal was not an option. It wasn't part of the debate that I was familiar with. I was responsible for a section of Hebron shortly after Baruch Goldstein massacred

Palestinians at the Tomb of the Patriarchs. It was like Sodom and Gomorrah there. But I never thought to say, "That's it. My soldiers and I refuse to go." You must realize that the apartheid in Hebron is worse than in any other Palestinian city, because there's a Jewish settlement in the heart of it. Do you know that Arabs are forbidden to walk on certain streets? That there are certain hours when the streets are off limits to Arabs? The racial separation there is unambiguous.

After the massacre, the city was licking its wounds, and the Arabs were trying to avenge their dead. This was before the Palestinian Authority was established, before there were arms in the territories. They came at us with whatever they could get their hands on, with knives and forks. It was really sad. Once, I was standing with another soldier, and someone ran toward us with a bucket. He threw what was in the bucket on the other soldier. It was acid. Then he started stabbing him, so we shot the attacker. These kinds of things happened all the time. There were furious, violent demonstrations there. We would shoot at them, and we injured many people. Were you to ask me how they lived in the midst of all this, I couldn't tell you. I really don't know. You'd stand there in the street and you wouldn't have any idea about their lives.

People don't really know what's happening there. If soldiers feel like having a shooting match all of a sudden, they'll use residential solar panels as targets. They won't think twice about the number of daily salaries that someone had to save up just to install them. People don't understand that it's apartheid. The settlers have fast lanes, and the Palestinians have five-hour traffic jams.

Another reason why people don't know what's happening is that the euphemism factory works overtime in Israel. When you hear some news report about a search, you have no idea what it actually means. A search means coming into a home at night, yanking people from their beds, pushing a family into a corner, and holding a gun to the father's head. The kid screams and pees in his pants, so the grandmother starts screaming too. You smack her, and threaten to silence her with a gun, so she won't wake up the whole neighborhood. After all, you have to search the neighbors' houses too.

I served for six years as a reserve soldier—mostly because of my friends, but also because I thought that if I didn't do this, a more violent, less sensitive soldier would do it in my place. At some point, I realized that I overestimated my ability to make a difference. The only difference between us was that I would let a little girl run and get her doll before demolishing her house, whereas another officer might not. My influence on the reality of occupation was negligible, while my physical presence there was critical to its implementation.

Most of the guys in Courage to Refuse tried to change the army from within for years. I also thought it was important to do the job myself instead of leaving it to my soldiers. Today I'm not willing to think along those lines. It's like saying, "If I don't want to steal, my friend will have to do it for me." That's a distortion of reality. We aren't co-workers in a factory. We aren't talking about work here. We're talking about committing crimes.

About two and a half years ago I had a conversation with my battalion commander. I told him that I wanted to stay in my unit, but that I wouldn't serve in the territories anymore. A month later, he called me in to tell me I was being transferred out of the unit. Things don't normally work like that. An outstanding officer valued by his soldiers isn't so easily dismissed. This was how the battalion commander chose to deal with what I had told him. He wanted to avoid a situation in which one of his officers refused to serve in front of his soldiers. A month later, I was placed in the home-front command. I went from an elite unit to the rearguard. At the time, I took it badly. On the home-front command, the chances to refuse were very small.

You ask me at what point my decision to refuse became apparent to me? Let's distinguish between the decision to refuse on a personal level, which crystallized over a few years, and the decision to sign the letter and turn my refusal into a political stand. January of 2002 was the turning point that propelled me into public refusal. It was because of the IDF spokesperson's lies about what happened in Rafah.

On the night of January 10, 2002, the IDF demolished sixty homes in Rafah in the southern Gaza Strip in one of those ground-clearing operations. The IDF spokesperson announced that the houses had been abandoned. But according to Israeli and Palestinian human rights organizations, the operation left 112 families homeless. It was on that day that I called Yaniv Iczkovitz to ask him what we should do. At this stage, I wasn't thinking of the letter as a call to withdraw from the territories. It was only later that the political ramifications of our refusal became apparent to me.

The state is not an entity that has to be served. It's a mechanism that's supposed to serve us. When the state commits crimes, your role as a citizen and guardian of democracy is to defy it. It should be remembered that the Nazis were also democratically elected.

Our call to refuse is an outcry about the state of our society. Unthinkable things are going on here. Nobody can deny the Palestinians their national aspirations. Personally, I'd like to see Israel establish a state for all its citizens in the future. I want a state that will respect the rights of the different groups that comprise it. As long as the occupation continues, we can't talk about equality. Does anyone in our government address the issue of inequality or the collapsing educational system? The bulk of the budget is allocated to security and settlements. When I hear the finance minister talk about allocating the territories more money, I say God help us. The economy is in crisis, with 11 percent unemployment, and the finance minister is talking about ear-marking more resources for bypass roads[2] and armored communities.

I have a hard time with these priorities. We are sick of reinforc-ing the messianic-nationalist aspirations of a privileged sector of the nation. Our call to stop oppressing another people is a battle over the character of the state. A state that conducts itself in keeping with morality is stronger than a state that deploys tanks to subdue children throwing stones.

CHACHAM: How do you see yourself in retrospect, as a soldier partici-pating in a practice that today you find shameful?

GROSSMAN: In the last few weeks I've been going over how I used to enter a village in the territories during the first Intifada. Once we entered a refugee camp. Someone spotted us and ran toward us with a big stone. We shot and killed him. The order to enter the camp was legal. That much was clear. We hadn't been there for two days, and we needed to see what was going on. We also needed to shoot him, because he was standing ten meters from us with a big stone in his hands. The military police conducted an investigation. Whenever someone's killed in the territories, they investigate it. After ten minutes of interrogation, we were told that our lives had been in danger, that everything would be fine, and that we would have nothing to worry about. Do you get it? I'm thinking how I killed a man, and the interrogator's thinking I've got nothing to worry about, that I won't get in trouble.

I can't live with it anymore. Something about the whole affair doesn't seem right to me. Everything was legal, but someone died. How did this happen? Why did I kill him? Why was I there? I was

2. Roads paved so settlers can circumvent populated Palestinian areas. Many of the roads being paved today were first begun during the Rabin government and extended during Barak's administration.

there legally, in a situation that enabled me to kill him legally. But the fact that the man died, that weighs on my conscience. Today I understand that I shouldn't have been there in the first place. Anyone whose home is invaded by armed men will pick up a stone to protect himself. I feel so sorry for the man that was killed. I'm not willing to put myself in these situations anymore. It took me years to realize that despite what the politicians and generals tell us, this is a war of choice, and we don't have to be there.

Today, I look at myself and ask, "Who was that officer?" Why was I there? Why wasn't I thinking? I wasn't 13 years old; I could already vote. I'm recalling a story about cruelty toward the local population, but it's also the story of my own cruelty.

How could I not see it? That's what blows my mind. It helps me understand the Holocaust. I see Germany right in front of me. And I hate being told that we shouldn't make the comparison. True, you can't compare systematic Nazi genocide with our own occupation regime. But you can compare the psychological processes that took place there and are taking place here among our soldiers and Israeli society in general. I want people to start making the comparison, because I've realized what incredible rationalizations you can make just to keep participating in the occupation. If you don't rationalize things as you go, you can't live with yourself.

The Israeli public makes these rationalizations every day to avoid what's really going on. That's exactly what happened in Germany. The Germans didn't want to see the chimney smoke. It was something that was happening at a distance, in Poland. They got up in the morning, went to work, and didn't know what was going on in the camps. Today, I understand this phenomenon on the level of the German civilian as well as on the level of the soldier in the Wehrmacht. To stop this rationalization requires courage, maturity, and awareness. I lived in ignorance. I'd be lying to you if I told you I was distraught as a soldier. I wasn't upset at all. Once you become conscious, though, you need the courage to deflate the myths you were raised on. You can't tear them down all at once. It takes years.

The hardest part has to do with my relationship to the other fighters, those who are my friends. If you haven't served in a combat unit, you can't understand how intense the comradeship is. The army counts on it and fosters it, and we enact it without realizing its ideological underpinnings. I have many friends who no longer speak to me. With those who still do talk to me, my relationships are tense. They know I have nothing to gain by my refusal to serve. On the contrary, they know it's a detriment to my career and family. They know I love the state, but they're mad at me. Some regard me as a cancer in the body politic. I'm not happy to have to refuse. Refusal is problematic, but the alternative is far worse.

With the passing of each month, I realize just how radical the stand I took really was in this militaristic state of never-ending wars. At first, I thought we had a consensus, that if we worked at it we could sway public opinion in our favor. I had the enthusiasm of Che Guevara. I thought I could move mountains. But I found out that it takes more than that to enact change. In the past three months, my understanding has become more pointed. Three months ago, I never imagined I would find myself marginalized. I thought that peripheral groups were irrelevant, because they're beyond the parameters of public discourse. Today, I understand that outsider groups mark the political horizon.

When I read the things I said when you and I first started talking, I laugh. I realize how defensive and apologetic I was. Today, I know that refusal is negligible. What really counts is ending the occupation. Getting there requires us to create a culture of civil disobedience in the tradition of Martin Luther King, Malcolm X, and Gandhi. They too were trampled on and even shot at. With all due modesty, we continue their legacy and offer it to the Israeli public. We don't know how influential our refusal will be, or where it will lead. But we mustn't give up. If we give up, we'll abandon the field to the other side. As long as we remain present, we will remain relevant. We are the writing on the wall. We will stay in the game until the last tank rolls out of the occupied territories.

CHAPTER SIX

Staff Sergeant (Res.) Shamai Leibowitz

Shamai Leibowitz lives near Tel Aviv in Givat Shmuel. At 32, he is tall and striking in his black skullcap. A lawyer and a sergeant in the armored corps, he calls for an uncompromising struggle for equality based on what he sees as true Judaism.

I met Shamai Leibowitz at the High Court of Justice during a petition to stop the IDF's assassination policy. The proceedings were postponed repeatedly, he explained to me, as though the court were trying to buy time or avoid the uncomfortable discussion altogether. It can neither rule in favor of the assassinations nor easily curtail the government's activities.

Shamai's background is unique. He is the grandson of the late Professor Yesha'ayahu Leibowitz, the Jewish religious thinker who begged Israel to relinquish control of the territories and end its calamitous occupation of other people's territory immediately following the 1967 war. Yesha'ayahu Leibowitz also urged soldiers to refuse service in the territories. In the generation between them, Shamai's late father was a professor of mathematics at Ben Gurion University in Beersheba, and his mother is an English teacher, translator, and writer.

Shamai Leibowitz, the grandson, went through a long process before he refused to serve in the occupied territories. The challenge was

a matter not of conscience but of breaking social codes and walking away from the norm.

———

LEIBOWITZ: On conscription day, when you enter the base you don't receive an order to shoot little boys and girls. It unfolds as you serve. You're sent to Gaza or Balata,[1] and you storm into a house. A kid runs away because he's scared of you. So you shoot and kill him. Then you say to yourself, "Wait a minute, I didn't want to kill children. This goes against my will."

Most soldiers don't understand that you can't be moral while serving in the occupied territories. There's no such thing as an "enlightened occupation." It's an oxymoron. You can't dominate people and deny them their rights in an enlightened way. Should you bomb their villages and then hand out candy? Should you say, "Sorry we bombed your village and killed five people; we were trying to kill Mahmoud Abbas, but we ended up killing a woman and her four children instead. Sorry for the mistake!" These types of things happen there every day.

CHACHAM: Your grandfather had an immense influence on many people, myself included. What influence did he have on your intellectual and moral development?

LEIBOWITZ: It would be incorrect to say that just because I grew up in my grandfather's company, I adopted his convictions. I disagree with him on many points. He contended that there's no connection between morality and Judaism, that a man can be religious, and adhere to the precepts of hand washing, food blessing, and daily prayer, and still

1. The largest Palestinian refugee camp in the West Bank, on the outskirts of Nablus.

support the occupation. I claim, however, that there is an inherent connection. A religious Jew must also adhere to the precepts of not oppressing non-Jews, not humiliating them, not detaining people without trial.

Precisely because I'm religious, I must oppose the occupation. The resistance to the occupation rises out of true Judaism, not the false religion spread by the followers of Gush Emunim.[2] As far as I'm concerned, they might as well eat pork. They spill blood in vain, they subjugate people, treat them like subhumans, forbid them to use the roads, force them to walk kilometers on foot, and then they go pray.

After all that, what are their prayers worth? The person who thinks his prayers are worth something when he fasts and atones on Yom Kippur[3] and then causes immeasurable suffering to millions of people is dead wrong. The prophets state that those who inflict suffering on the weak take God's name in vain; there is no greater sin than desecrating God's name.

There's a saying in the Talmud: "In the place where blasphemy occurs, one need not show respect for the rabbis." In other words, one may criticize them. With all due respect to my rabbis, they are promoting sacrilege. I say this about the moderates too, because they haven't condemned the occupation. They've only gone as far as to say that they'd be willing to reach a territorial compromise when the Arabs are "obedient and compliant."

The Jewish precepts set forth by the prophets of Israel state that you don't have to wait until you beat your enemy into submission. Before everything else, you must prevent injustice. You must create peace by treating every human being and every nation with equality and respect. That's the principal obligation.

Of course I'd also like to see a peace settlement. But there can be

---

2. Religious-nationalist messianic founders of the settlers movement.
3. Jewish Day of Atonement, the culmination of the High Holy Days.

no peace between occupier and occupied; it's almost like asking for a peace agreement between rapist and victim while the rape is being carried out. First, the occupation must end, because it's a moral crime. After that, we can start talking about long-term arrangements.

CHACHAM: When did you decide to refuse?

LEIBOWITZ: A few days ago, I found a letter I had written to my battalion commander in 1993. I told him I could not take part in an operation I'd been called up for in Gaza. I said I opposed the Israeli occupation and the oppression it entails. My refusal to serve in Gaza was not a refusal to serve in the army altogether. I asked him to transfer me so I could serve elsewhere. The battalion commander agreed and sent me to the Egyptian border. Since then, I have not been called up to serve in the territories.

What I wrote in 1993 could have been written today. When you subjugate three million people and deny them basic civil rights, the situation inevitably leads to violence. Violence begets terror, and terror begets more violence.

CHACHAM: What about your education? Where did you go to school?

LEIBOWITZ: I studied at a yeshiva[4] in Gush Etzion.[5] The injustice of our very presence there pained me. I had a hard time with the fact that we had a swimming pool, while our neighbors not only didn't have a swimming pool, they didn't have drinking water or roads, nothing. The settlers with their fancy villas don't seem to mind it at all. You have to be callous to live like that while you ignore the suffering all around you. It's un-Jewish.

4. A Jewish religious educational institution.
5. A group of settlements between Jerusalem and Hebron.

For five years I swam in the pool and drove on roads that Palestinians are forbidden to set foot on. And I voted, knowing full well that all around me people don't have the right to vote. They have no sovereignty.

CHACHAM: I look around me and see very few people capable of breaking the dominant Israeli mode of thinking and conception of reality. I wonder, can we liberate ourselves from this mental stagnation?

LEIBOWITZ: Education is the key. That is, a proper education about human rights, liberty, respect, equality, commitment to the poor, the widow, the orphan, and the non-Jew. Yes, the non-Jew. As it is written, "When a stranger sojourns with you in your land, you shall not do him wrong. The stranger who sojourns with you shall be to you as the native among you, and you shall love him as yourself; for you were strangers in the land of Egypt."[6]

CHACHAM: You use the term "stranger" to refer to the Palestinians, who are actually native to this land! This seems to demonstrate how the nationalist narrative is so deeply ingrained in us. Perhaps if our education were different and taught us that the Palestinians were not "strangers" but indigenous inhabitants, our whole perception of the political situation would be different.

LEIBOWITZ: Our education has become very nationalistic in the past twenty or thirty years. It reinforces a sense of persecution and the threat of annihilation, and it says that we have to protect ourselves with a strong state and army. The educational system in Israel ingrains a sense of paranoia, saying that the whole world is always against us.

This kind of education emphasizes living by the sword at the

---

6. *Leviticus* 19:33–34.

expense of our values. While in exile, the Jews concerned themselves with social, ethical, and spiritual questions such as charity, caring for the sick and aged, and studying the Torah. Once we gained our independence as a nation, our educational system neglected these issues in favor of nationalism—and, dare I say it, the sanctity of arms.

CHACHAM: Do you think that the Bible was employed to justify nationalistic beliefs?

LEIBOWITZ: There are many examples. In the name of our divine right to the land, the settlers justify their fascist, fanatical ideology by distorting the Bible.

For instance, Abraham and his nephew Lot reached the land God had promised Abraham. Both men had cattle and property, and their shepherds quarreled over areas of pasture. Abraham suggested a compromise for sharing the land. In order not to spite Lot with God's promise of the land, which he could have done, Abraham preferred giving up land, saying: "Let there be no strife between you and me, and between your herdsmen and my herdsmen; for we are kinsmen. Is not the whole land before you? Separate yourself from me. If you take the left hand, then I will go to the right; or if you take the right hand, then I will go to the left."[7] In other words, choose your spot, and we'll parcel out the territory.

That's also what Abraham did with Abimelech when they quarreled over the wells. Abimelech was not a righteous man, but instead of fighting him and killing his slaves, which Abraham was in a position to do, he preferred to compromise with him. They made an agreement, and that's how the city of Beersheba came to be. In other words, the first Hebrew city in the world was formed as a covenant of peace

7. *Genesis* 13:8–9.

between Abimelech and Abraham, who preferred to reach an agreement instead of denying Abimelech his rights.

For years, the religious educational system deliberately purged this idea from their textbooks. The Rabbis made sure students were not exposed to it.

The settlers' attitude is diametrically opposed to Abraham's. They think the Palestinians don't deserve water, electricity, or anything that can be included under the rubric of independence: a state, an economy, industry, political rights, a flag, or an anthem.

Nationalist urges have led our teachers and rabbis to shamelessly distort the Bible. They isolate specific verses about bravery, war, and occupation. They transmit these decontextualized and essentialized verses to thousands of students as though they were the core values of Judaism.

One Talmudic sage taught his students that because Jacob hurt Esau, and then Esau threatened to kill him, Esau would always hate Jacob. The lesson was titled: Esau maligns Jacob. It must be remembered that the author of this particular lesson was projecting what he saw around him, Jews suffering persecution at the hands of the Romans. To teach that to the young in Israel today very seriously distorts Judaism. I've heard the nationalist rabbis in the synagogues: Just as we are taught that Esau will always hate Jacob, the Palestinians will always hate Jews. If that isn't incitement, then I don't know what is. Instead of teaching children the actual text, they teach them nationalist propaganda.

When you read the actual text, what you find is that, despite the conflict that raged between Jacob and Esau, at the end of the day they made peace.[8] They divided the land between them, even though Esau was the culprit, the one who threatened Jacob with murder, the "ter-

---

8. *Genesis* 33:4–10.

rorist" if you will. The Bible teaches us that Esau was also a human being with compassion and sympathy, who, when respected and granted his rights, preferred peace. The Bible's perspective is not one-sided, and humanity overcomes vengeance. It's a terrific story!

The lesson in this story, spread over three whole chapters of Genesis, is that in the end you need to make peace with your enemies. You can't discriminate against them and simultaneously make peace. First, you must treat them as equals. Then divide up the land and reap the benefits of reconciliation.

Why have I brought up this text as an example? To demonstrate how easy it is to distort and convey a textual interpretation that bears no relation to its biblical source. I hear friends of mine say, "Why do you want to make peace with the Arabs? They can't be trusted; they'll always want to murder us," "We can't give up the Sinai," or "We can't give up South Lebanon." And today, "We can't withdraw from Balata and Rafah." It's always the same motif: Esau maligns Jacob. We see how these religious educators are not only warmongers, they are blasphemers who don't hesitate to distort the Bible to justify their sinister nationalist teachings.

CHACHAM: You place a great deal of the blame on religious instruction. But it could be argued that the problem isn't typical of the religious system alone. Is the secular world any different?

LEIBOWITZ: Our judges are also guilty of perpetuating the occupation. The High Court justices are the worst. They've legitimized assassinations, administrative detentions, expulsions, and house demolitions for thirty-five years, policies unheard of in a democratic state. And all in the name of "security."

Benjamin Franklin said, "They that can give up essential liberty to obtain a little temporary safety deserve neither liberty nor safety." The judges stripped our country of liberty, sticking the fig leaf of state security in its place! And just as Franklin suggested, they've contributed to making our people less secure. Because of their wish to justify the state's actions, our security has deteriorated to the lowest level since the establishment of the state.

CHACHAM: How can a judicial system internalize the dominant ideology so thoroughly?

LEIBOWITZ: They never received a proper legal education. If they had, they would have concluded that when the authorities order the destruction of houses and the detention of people without trial, it isn't the judge's job to sanction that. In a democracy, judges aren't supposed to represent the authorities. Everybody deserves due process, even the most dangerous terrorists and conspirators. If they don't understand this, they don't deserve to be judges.

I would compare them to Ahab's judges.[9] The evil king of Israel, Ahab, and his wife, Jezebel, prosecuted Naboth the Jezreelite for refusing to obey Ahab's orders. Ahab asked Naboth for his vineyard in exchange for either money or another tract of land. But Naboth refused to part with his forefathers' vineyard. So they brought Naboth before their High Court, and the court no doubt issued a detailed ruling that, when it came to state security, there was no choice but to violate his rights.

So in the case of Naboth, who disturbed the public order by his refusal to obey the king, it was okay to ignore his human rights. After his conviction, he was stoned to death. And the public bought it; after all,

9. 1 *Kings* 21.

there was a trial, there were witnesses, a prosecutor, an advocate, a learned ruling, and so forth. He was deemed a "security threat," and then it was very easy to sway public opinion in favor of assassinating him.

The story of Naboth is an analogy for the corruption of our judicial system. We, too, have witnesses; a prosecution; an association for civil rights in Israel, B'Tselem;[10] and defense attorneys who represent Palestinians. It's all a bluff, because the judges are part of the system. And they team up with the prosecution to perpetrate terrible injustices.

This absolute devotion to the regime is wrong and dangerous. You won't find a single prosecutor who'll stand up and say, "I won't do this!" They're like those automatic drink machines: the money goes in and the drink comes out. You stick a prosecutor in a courtroom, and automatically he or she defends the regime. I would like the attorney general and the state legal adviser to read the story of Naboth's trial. They should be ashamed of themselves. As Jews, I expect a lot more of them. Instead of defending the corrupt occupation regime, they should have cried out, "Cease to do evil!"[11]

And the judges take their cues from Ahab, King of Israel, and his judges instead of heeding Elijah the Prophet, who condemned Ahab for his bogus trial. Two whole chapters of the Bible—and hundreds of commentaries and essays relating to them—are dedicated to admonishing us to avoid this kind of behavior.

I mean, why do they tell us that Naboth had a vineyard and the wicked Israeli king came and took it? And why tell us the whole story of the trial? Why should we care? It's not the vineyard that's at stake, nor is it Naboth; it's the principle. Elijah the Prophet wanted to demonstrate that the regime always tries to corrupt the judicial system. But I must add that there are a few judges, very few, who are courageous enough to stand up to the regime—the late Judge Chaim Cohen, for example.

10. The Israeli Organization for Human Rights in the Occupied Territories.
11. *Isaiah* 1:16.

CHACHAM: How do you interpret the story in today's context?

LEIBOWITZ: The regime has an interest in the occupation, and our judges are willing to corrupt the legal system to enable it. Tomorrow the regime will have an interest in throwing out all the leftists, and the judges will find ways to corrupt the legal process in order to do so.

Today the regime assassinates Palestinians in cold blood. After each "liquidation," they issue a press release announcing that the targeted man was a "security threat." Nobody asks questions, and the judges sit in silence. Tomorrow they'll start doing the same thing to Jews. They'll say, "Uri Avneri[12] collaborated with Arafat. That's why we liquidated him." In the end, they'll get to me. It sounds unreal, but it's a lot closer than people realize.

The judges prostitute the legal system to please the regime. In the words of Isaiah, "How the faithful city has become a harlot."[13] The judges know very well that we exercise state terror, but they gloss over their justification of every evil deed with the magic words: "maintaining the public order," "state security," and "the public interest." There are credible testimonies about war crimes, but the judges will not hear them. How else can you explain that all of the appeals to the High Court of Justice that were filed on behalf of plaintiffs seeking to counter the occupation have been rejected? It's just like Ahab and Jezebel's judges. In the words of Ecclesiastes, "In the place of justice, even there was wickedness."[14]

CHACHAM: What are the legal implications of the practices that the military carries out in the occupied territories?

---

12. Israeli peace activist and former member of the Knesset, known for his longstanding association with Arafat.

13. *Isaiah* 1:21–23.

14. *Ecclesiastes* 3:15–17.

LEIBOWITZ: Liquidations are extra-judicial killings. Every soldier must know that by virtue of being in the territories he is complicit in assassinations. And every soldier who aids or abets the army is implicated, because he knows that the army carries out assassinations in the territories. Even in war there are rules of engagement, and people are not to be executed without a trial. Extra-judicial slayings are a war crime. So every soldier who serves in the territories unwittingly becomes an accomplice to these war crimes and has the legal right to state that he refuses to take part in them.

The IDF has used innocent Palestinians as human shields. And those who refused were simply shot at point-blank range. And the most sickening part of this is that the Supreme Court condoned these war crimes. That's why I'm in favor of bringing the justices to trial before the International Criminal Court. The IDF has prevented ambulances from evacuating the wounded, and hundreds of injured Palestinians have been left to die and rot in refugee camps and cities. The IDF has shot people for violating curfew by going out to buy a loaf of bread after being locked up for four days with another fifty people in a single room. These crimes have witnesses, and that's why the army bars journalists from entering to see what's really going on. They buried people in mass graves in some of these cities and camps. It's horrific.

I know a combat pilot who refused to bomb civilians in the Lebanon War. So what did the army do? They stopped sending him on those assignments. And it's a shame he wasn't indicted, because then he would have stood trial. And Israel's practice of killing Palestinians would be put on trial and given wide media exposure. I expect the Apache gunship and F16 fighter pilots to refuse their orders and demand a trial, to resist the army's attempt to ground them on their bases while other hooligans do the dirty work in their place.

CHACHAM: You encourage refuseniks to stand trial, whereas the usual procedure doesn't entail trial. In the Israeli army, your commander sends you to prison as part of a disciplinary procedure rather than sending you to face a formal court martial. These proceedings are notoriously short. There are no lawyers, no witnesses, and the commander simply disciplines the soldier for refusing an order and places him or her in military prison for 28 days.

LEIBOWITZ: I call on them to hire a lawyer who will bring the Fourth Geneva Convention to the court's attention. Let's see what the court does with that. I call on people to do it, but I don't see enough men who are prepared to.[15] The refuseniks must understand that if they go to jail without a trial, the IDF won't budge even if a hundred refusers are incarcerated. As far as the struggle goes, it's meaningless. Only by demanding a fair trial will they get their point across. And they need representation. You need to know how to state your claims, see how the army responds, and know how to tell the army their rejoinder is inadequate.

In one case, a soldier asked me to defend him. He managed to get a trial, but his commanders deceived him and told him he had no right to legal representation. They promptly threw him in jail. In order to justify the occupation, they lie, deceive, corrupt the legal system, and throw Jews in jail without habeas corpus, which they've done for years to Palestinians.

---

15. At the time of this interview, one of the initiators of the Courage to Refuse letter, David Zonsheine, had been jailed for 35 days for refusing to carry out a tour of duty in the occupied territories. He asked to be given a full military trial to argue his case. Just as with a few other signatories before him, the army turned him down. Then Zonsheine petitioned the Israeli High Court of Justice to force the army to try him. On December 30, 2002, the High Court ruled against Zonsheine and sentenced him to prison for refusing his call-up.

CHACHAM: Are you calling for a more militant form of refusal?

LEIBOWITZ: I call on all soldiers to refuse to commit war crimes and to demand a full military trial. I call on them to abandon their bases, to refuse to repair tanks, artillery units, warplanes, helicopters, and every other piece of war machinery used against civilians. I urge soldiers to open the gates of all the detention centers, where thousands of Palestinians are incarcerated without trial for months. At the same time, I also call on them to state their willingness to protect the state of Israel within its democratic borders.[16]

The claim that this will signal the end of the army and the demise of the state is utter nonsense. Historically, no society has collapsed because a group of people within it said they refused to commit an evil act. If a society collapsed, it would be because a group of people went out and committed destructive acts.

The army is so central to the Israeli experience that it's hard for people to come out against it and tell their commanders, "You, my commander, are a party to immoral and criminal acts." That's why the refusal movement needs strong support from American Jewry. I'm talking about economic support and media coverage.

CHACHAM: When you call for resistance to the army and question the adequacy of the judicial system, do you take into consideration everything you have to lose?

LEIBOWITZ: Yes, I'm aware of the possibility that tomorrow some judge may rule against all my clients because he read somewhere that attorney Leibowitz called for refusal.

16. These are the borders decided upon by the international community after the 1948 war (see Maps, Figure 1).

But one of the major precepts in Judaism is: "You shall not be afraid of the face of man, for the judgment is God's."[17] Israel, as a democratic state, is collapsing before our very eyes. Our ruling dictatorship has plunged Israel into an ongoing bloodbath that must be stopped. I am very worried about Israel's fate. That's why I have to put this issue above my personal goals. Just yesterday I heard that a rabbi in my community attacked me in my absence and compared me to a kapo.[18]

A few days ago I brought a letter to my synagogue that was written by Itai Haviv, one of the Courage to Refuse officers. He explained his reasons for refusing, saying that for 35 years in the occupation he chased after children in alleyways, he searched for subversive material between blankets and mattresses, he heard babies crying, he yanked people out of bed to erase slogans from walls, he enforced curfews, he confiscated ID cards, he shot demonstrators, he set up a lookout on the roof of a bakery on Gaza's main street, he believed in the "no-choice" war. "We left no stone unturned in our search for peace," he quoted Ehud Barak as saying. And, at the same time, we built 100 settlements and put 200,000 settlers in them. We lost fighters, mothers, children, and all for peace. For 35 years, a black flag[19] has been flying over our heads, and we've refused to see it.

One of the members of the congregation in my synagogue stood up and said, "Somebody brought an abominable thing in here. I ask that this person never do it again and not show his face here anymore."

Their nationalism is so extreme that they hate Jews who don't share their nationalism. They hate the Palestinians for wanting their own state, and they hate the Jewish leftists for not sharing their fanatical vision of a "Greater Israel." To this day, I don't think that the secular public has registered this fact. It is the religious public that is

---

17. *Deuteronomy* 1:17.
18. Jewish "headman" collaborator in the Nazi concentration camps.
19. See Chapter 2, note 2.

responsible for the current bloodshed. I pray with this public, I study with it, I live among them; I know what I'm talking about.

The borders of the State of Israel need to be fixed along the 1967 lines. Then the settlers need to be compensated. Once the state decides where its permanent boundaries are, if the settlers want to emigrate from Israel to live in the Palestinian State we should let them. It's their right. Just as it's their right to emigrate to the United States.

As for the issue of a Jewish majority, I don't see how we can forsake our basic democratic tenets just to preserve it. I say, either defend democracy all the way or give up the idea of a Jewish state. But this is not going to be easy. Arabophobia is rampant. So many people are afraid of the Arab-Israeli population growth. This reminds me of a famous wicked king who had the same fear about the Jews in his land. These were exactly his words: "Come on, let us deal with them wisely, lest they multiply, and it come to pass that when war breaks out they join also onto our enemies, and fight against us."[20] That was Pharaoh, King of Egypt, and it led him to the following cruel conclusion: "Every son that is born to the Hebrews you shall cast into the Nile."[21]

The principle of a state for the Jewish people is dear to me. But not a state that looks like Pharaoh's Egypt.

As for the right of return for the Palestinians, it must be acknowledged. Most important, we must ask forgiveness for the injustices we committed in 1948. We were so used to being persecuted that we forgot about the power of forgiveness. Apologizing is fundamental to Judaism. What disaster will befall us if our leaders recognize the sin of expelling the refugees and apologize for it? Judaism teaches every person to say, "We have become guilty, we have betrayed, we have robbed."[22] Whoever recites that, and doesn't understand what we've

20. *Exodus* 1:10.
21. *Exodus* 1:22.
22. From the Yom Kippur prayers of repentance.

done to hundreds of thousands of refugees, is praying like a robot. His prayers are worthless. Let him do yoga instead. The problem is that so many Jews have lost their Jewish soul and can't even say, "I'm sorry" anymore. We must understand that apologizing is the first step toward reconciliation.

Before dealing with any other phenomena in Israeli society—gender inequality, failing education, road rage—we must put all our energies into resisting the occupation. The occupation has destroyed our judicial system, our educational system, and, worst of all, our Jewish religion. I sense real despondency on the left. We've fought the occupation for so many years, and it's gotten even worse. The truth is that the occupation will end only when a majority of loyal soldiers refuse to take part in it. That will happen when members of the Knesset, judges, professors, rabbis, writers, and artists all call on IDF troops to refuse to dominate and oppress the Palestinian nation. When that happens, you'll see that the occupation regime will collapse, and a true Jewish society, a society of justice, fairness, and compassion, will be formed.

CHAPTER SEVEN

Lieutenant (Res.) Yuval Lotem

Yuval Lotem, a 45-year-old filmmaker and father of one, lives in Kfar Shmaryahu, an affluent town north of Tel Aviv. He was born in Haifa to a family with a strong footing in the country. They were Ashkenazi socialists, Labor-party supporters, the people who have benefited from falling on the "right" side of the ethnic divide. Nonetheless, he does not see himself as someone who has enjoyed any special privileges.

Yuval has refused to serve in Israeli-occupied territory many times. Twice, he has been imprisoned for doing so. The first time he refused his orders was during the Lebanon War. As a 25-year-old lieutenant, he would not take part in that war. He was not jailed but was merely transferred to another unit. After this initial episode, he went on to refuse service in the occupied Palestinian territories. Each time, the army threatened him with imprisonment, but in the end they always transferred him somewhere else.

During the first Intifada, Yuval refused to serve in Gaza, and he was finally sentenced to 28 days in a military prison. Several years later, he refused a tour of duty in the Megiddo prison. Though Megiddo is inside the Green Line, Yuval did not feel he could serve because Palestinian administrative detainees were held there. Again, he found himself sentenced to 28 days in the brig.

—

LOTEM: My parents, who were born here, were from pioneering families. They came here to realize the Zionist dream. I grew up in a working-class home. I always earned a living with my hands through construction, locksmith, and electricity work.

My uncle was killed in one of the wars, so my family was very upset when I refused. I tried to explain to them that my refusal would keep others from dying, but it didn't go over very well. In family gatherings now, I prefer to keep quiet. Family is more important to me than anything else.

My late father was a model for humanity. He was open-minded. He was a seaman, and he loved poetry. He taught me to look at everything with a critical eye. I was raised to be confident, to feel safe and secure. That's why I'm a self-assured, optimistic guy who thinks that in the end everything's gonna be all right.

At the age of 18, I went into the army with the belief that I was going to do battle for our existence. I wanted to serve in an elite unit that's hard to get into. I insisted. I appealed to several committees, was finally admitted, and served with great enthusiasm. Even today, with all the critical awareness I've gained over the years, I would still take the combat route. I don't believe that the state should give up its capacity for deterrence. No state should. But, at the same time, I believe everything should be done to avoid having to use it. I'm not a pacifist. I'm willing to fight for my home. Everybody has the right to self-defense. But I won't participate in encroaching on someone else's home.

Six months after my release from the army as a regular conscript, I went to South Africa looking for romance. I traveled. I made a living as an electrician and a construction worker. Far from home, I began to distance myself from the social conventions I was raised on, and I took a second look at everything. I met Germans there, and we discussed World War II and the Holocaust. I remember one of them talking about the Nazis, saying "Everyone was like that." Then I understood that "everyone" is not an excuse. So what if everyone's doing it? Don't follow along! "Everyone" is not a valid argument.

When I returned from South Africa straight into the Lebanon War, I already had a budding political consciousness. I was a 25-year-old lieutenant in the reserves, and I refused to participate in the war, but I wasn't jailed. Ten years later, in 1993, I refused again. This time I was jailed. I was studying film at Tel Aviv University and working as a taxi driver. I was supposed to serve in Gaza. This was back when Labor was in power, and Rabin was still prime minister. A lot of people were mad at me: "How can you refuse when they're talking about peace?" But this line of reasoning didn't justify serving in the territories.

Sure, Israel had given up Gaza, but the occupation continued unhindered: border closures, killings, the oppression of a civilian population. I wasn't willing to put myself in a situation where I might have to shoot some kid who threw a stone at me. I couldn't picture forcing my way into homes, wearing an officer's uniform, and pointing a weapon around. It would mean that I dominated them by force. I was very optimistic about the peace process.

CHACHAM: How could you have been optimistic? You saw the occupation continuing. On the one hand, they signed peace agreements, and on the other hand Gaza was under closure. As a direct result, hundreds of thousands of Gazan laborers who depended on the Israeli economy for their living were denied work. Gaza suddenly found itself hermetically sealed and isolated.

LOTEM: I get my optimism from the signals ahead. After years of inertia on the Palestinian issue, the train had finally started moving. I continue to believe it will move. Unfortunately, it is blood, death, and destruction that will set it in motion. When the blood overflows, the wheels will start turning again. They'll start slowly at first, and with terrible difficulty. But they will move.

In 1997 I refused again and was sentenced to 28 days in prison. When I got the order, I spoke to an officer in my unit and told him I wouldn't go to the West Bank. The officer said they'd sentence me for refusal. Then another officer suggested that they send me someplace else. I asked the liaison officer to tell me where. She said, "Inside the Green Line, Megiddo Prison." I knew that Megiddo was where the administrative detainees were held. These are the Palestinian prisoners who have been incarcerated without a trial and are denied letters, phone calls, and visits. I told her I wouldn't go to Megiddo Prison. The 19-year-old liaison officer looked at me in astonishment and said, "What's with you? We're a democratic state, and everything in Megiddo is consistent with the rule of law." There was no point in arguing with this naive young woman. I went to Megiddo because I didn't want to be considered AWOL.[1]

I guess the battalion commander at Megiddo knew about my past refusals and thought he could break me. He claimed that the prisoners were all terrorists, potential suicide bombers. He said that he'd help me out, that all I had to do was sit in the "war room" and patrol the outer camp with a jeep, that I wouldn't have to come into contact with the prisoners.

I told him that Megiddo was an integral part of the occupation, and it made no difference whether it was inside the Green Line. I told him that there might be stone-throwers among the prisoners, and there was no justification for jailing them. If my home were subject to an

---

1. Army acronym for "absent without leave."

occupying army, I'd do exactly what they did. I told him that the most disturbing part was that there were prisoners there who had been incarcerated for years without any charges being brought against them. I added that not only were the jailers criminals, the entire system was unacceptable, and that there was nothing for me to do there as long as I did not intend to be an accomplice to a crime.

Upon his release from military lockup in July 1997, Yuval Lotem received a letter from Megiddo Prison. It was written, in English, by an administrative detainee. The script was so small that it had to be magnified in order to be deciphered:

A LETTER TO AN ANONYMOUS SOLDIER

A small item in the *Al-Quds* newspaper dated July 8, 1997 read: "Israeli soldier who refused to serve in Megiddo Prison sentenced to military lockup." The item, which totaled eight lines, reported that an officer with the rank of lieutenant said, "I prefer to be a prisoner in jail than the jailer of political prisoners incarcerated without a trial."

Who are you?

Who are you, officer?

I want to write to you, but first I need to know who you are. I need to know what motivated you to do what you did. I need to know how you arrived at this principled, conscientious decision. How is it that you opted to rebel in this most unique, unexpected way?

Who are you?

What's your name? Where do you live? What do you do? How old are you? Do you have children? Do you love the sea? What books do you read? And what are you doing this very moment in the cell in which you are imprisoned? Do you have enough cigarettes? Does anyone there identify with you? Are you asking yourself, "Was it worth it?" What feelings fill your soul, trapped between the bare walls closing in around you? Do I know you? Have we ever met? Can you see the moon and the stars from your cell window? Have your ears adjusted to the clanging of heavy keys, the screeching of locks, the banging of metal doors? What did they tell you in your court martial, and what did you reply?

Do you see fields of wheat and oat swaying in the wind in your sleep? Do you see plains of sunflowers that feast your eyes with shades of yellow, green, and black, and the sun tans you, and you smile in your sleep, and the walls come tumbling down, and an anonymous man waves to you from afar?

Who are you, lieutenant?

Why do you attribute so much importance to the issue of administrative detainees?

Do you really hold my freedom so dear?

Would the role of jailer have broken you? Just a week, or two, or three at the most, and you would have finished your reserve duty, and returned to your civilian life.

Indeed, you could have kept silent, conquered your anger, kept your feelings to yourself. You could have been a polite jailer, treated the detainees with courtesy, and been humane. What would have happened to you had you done so?

So who are you?

How do the wardens treat you? Does your wife visit you, maybe your girlfriend, your mother, or your children? Do you write letters? To whom? How do you begin a letter to a woman you love? Do you think about me? What does my freedom mean to you? What, in your eyes, is the meaning of freedom in general? Isn't "state security" important to you? And what if I'm a real terrorist? What would you say then?

Aren't you regretful? Didn't some doubt creep in when they said, "They're dangerous, they belong to Hamas, to Islamic Jihad, to the Popular Front"? Don't you trust our security services? Do you really think we'd throw innocent people into jail?"

So who are you?

Are you asleep now? Or are you lying on your back, staring at the

---

2. Various Palestinian resistance movements.

ceiling, deep in thought? What color are your eyes? Are you short or tall? What makes you happy and what makes you angry? Do they allow you to have books? Do they give you the daily paper? What do you see in your jailer's eyes? Do you smile often? Do you hear the birds singing at dawn? Do the army blankets irritate you? Will peace ever come? Will Oslo bring peace? Is the Likud interested in peace? Is the Labor party interested in peace?

Anonymous lieutenant, be your name what it may, sleep well. The peaceful sleep of a man with a clean conscience. I will soon know your name, and then I will write you a long letter, a letter from one prisoner to another. I will open my letter with "Hello, dear" and end it with "Yours truly,"

Imad Saba
July 13, 1997

Imad Saba was detained on December 12, 1995, with no charges brought against him, without standing trial, and with no limitations on the length of his arrest. The authorities' claim against him was that he was active with the Popular Front for the Liberation of Palestine, a militant Palestinian resistance group, and therefore posed a threat to regional security. In May 1997, while Saba was in detention, the Israeli human rights organization B'Tselem reported that 249 Palestinian administrative detainees were being held in degraded, camp-like conditions, forced to sleep in tents, and exposed to the elements. Until his arrest, Saba had been director general of the Bisan Institute for Research and Development in Ramallah and a lecturer at Bir Zeit University.

Saba, an intellectual who wrote prolifically from prison about the likes of Paul Auster and Noam Chomsky, was awarded a graduate fellowship at a research institute in The Hague. He asked the army to release him from administrative detention so he could pursue his studies. His request was denied. Finally, after many months of negotiation, Saba was released in a deal worked out between his lawyer and the General Security Services. The night of his release, he was deported to Holland, despite the fact that he was never charged with a crime.

———

LOTEM: After reading Imad Saba's letter, and an article about him in the newspaper, I decided that I wanted to meet him. In the paper, there was a photo of Imad holding his baby girl, Dina. We both have daughters the same age. But he was prevented from caring for his daughter for two years. It was important to me that Imad and his friends know there were Israelis who didn't think like the young soldiers who jailed them. That there were Israelis who believed that our two peoples could live together honorably.

Following his release from military lockup, Yuval Lotem contacted Imad Saba, and they formed an acquaintanceship that continues to this day. In addition to Imad, Yuval befriended other Palestinian political activists. Most of them are former administrative detainees.

Among them is Ali Jaradat, a spokesperson for the Popular Front for the Liberation of Palestine,[3] whose members have been held in administrative detention for their accused involvement in the assassination of Rehavam Zeevi.[4] Yuval Lotem is in contact with Jaradat's family and has visited them in Ramallah and Qalqilya. Because of the present situation, he can reach them only by telephone nowadays. Ramallah and Qalqilya, like other Palestinian cities, are subject to ongoing closures and aerial bombardment. Yuval can hear the barrage when he calls to check on his Palestinian friends and their families.

Yuval Lotem also sheltered an illegal worker from Gaza in his home for several weeks. Following one of the suicide bombings, the IDF sealed off the Gaza Strip. The worker, whom Lotem knew, couldn't get back to Gaza until the blockade was eased.

——

LOTEM: When he went back to Gaza, people there couldn't believe that an Israeli would do such a thing. But I didn't see it as something heroic. After all, they don't execute Jews for refusing to serve in the territories or for harboring Palestinian laborers.

3. The PFLP (Popular Front for the Liberation of Palestine) is "a Marxist political movement working toward establishing a democratic state on the land of historic Palestine, where all people can live as equal citizens regardless of race, religion, color, or sex," according to their official website. The IDF, Amnesty International, and Human Rights Watch have accused them of planning suicide bombings.

4. The former Israeli minister of tourism who was killed on October 17, 2001. A right-wing politician, he advocated the transfer of the Palestinians.

CHACHAM: Given that Saba and his comrades were detained for membership in the Popular Front, what do you know about their group? Did you discuss it? Did you talk about the Popular Front's ideology?

LOTEM: I never ask Imad about his activism. I don't feel comfortable doing so, though I understand they need to fight for their homes just as I'm prepared to fight for mine. I don't have any problem with that. I would also resist my occupier. When I received Imad's letter, it didn't strike me as something a man who wanted to kill Jews would write. I don't believe he would bomb a kindergarten. Anyway, he was never tried because they never found any evidence with which to charge him or the other administrative detainees. Saba objected to the Oslo process, and he published articles to that effect. A day or two before handing Ramallah over to the Palestinian Authority, Israel rounded up all the Oslo opponents and put them in administrative detention.

CHACHAM: Since Saba was part of the opposition to Arafat, it's very likely that he expressed the concern of the Palestinian opposition. They felt that the Oslo agreement wasn't going to bring about the independence and sovereignty the Palestinians were hoping for. They saw it as a reoccupation, this time under the control of Chairman Arafat's policemen.

LOTEM: I know a little about the Popular Front. I know they envision a single democratic state for all citizens, a state that sees its subjects as equals regardless of race or religion. It's a progressive idea whose time has yet to come. Meanwhile, we need to realize the vision of two states. But I didn't have political arguments with Imad and his friends. Once, in Ramallah, Ali Jaradat and I joked about three states: a Muslim one, a Jewish one, and a normal one.

CHACHAM: Since you're nonpolitical as you've stated time and again, how do you define your reasons for refusing?

LOTEM: I didn't refuse in order to change the world, but so I could sleep at night, so I wouldn't have a problem looking in the mirror. Refusing was a selfish act on my part. I didn't use to feel comfortable admitting this, but I've always known that I was doing it for me and me alone. Refusal strikes me as a very small deed. Refusal is connecting with one's self. Men in general, and Israeli men in particular, have a very hard time connecting with themselves. The minute you listen to your inner voice, you know what's good and what's bad.

As for the refusenik movement, I think it needs to be proactive. I'd be happy to push it along. The movement needs to transgress the limits of the law. We need to send an unambiguous message calling on people to refuse, and not just asking for their support. This will provoke a counter-call for legal proceedings to be initiated against us; it's unavoidable. The problem is that our movement is afraid of breaking away from the pack. But it will remain marginal if it doesn't sound the call to resist.

CHACHAM: Can you recall any milestones on your way to refusal?

LOTEM: Some things lodged in my memory. Between my enthusiastic conscription and my decision to refuse, I wasn't really aware of them until they added up to a critical mass. In Gaza, I saw some kids who were afraid of me. They moved to the side when I passed by them. I smiled at one of them. Much to my surprise, he didn't smile back. It took me a while to see myself through his eyes. I still remember that boy's eyes. Then I saw South African kids with the same look. That's when I started to comprehend that I'm on the ruling side.

That's why I'm raising my daughter to have humane and democratic values. I want her to understand that she belongs to a bigger tribe than the one that defines itself according to racial criteria. A humane approach can't be transmitted in words. If you're a humanist, your children will absorb it too. If you aren't, all the words in the world won't help. She knows my Palestinian friends' children. But I don't want her to hate the settlers, either. I think about the fact that they'll have to be evacuated, and I feel empathy toward them. Their pain is real. We mustn't forget that.

CHACHAM: Are you optimistic?

LOTEM: The state is moving toward a sane solution. True, it's hard to see the progress. In Qalqilya, they can't feel it because they're still dominated by Israelis. But we must remember that ten years ago talking about a Palestinian state was considered treasonous, and today everybody's talking about it. I talk about it with all kinds of people. Even with Likud[5] supporters. I know, because I have friends who aren't on the left and don't belong to the Ashkenazi mainstream. I'm a part of my society; I'm not an outsider. I'm an officer in the paratroopers, not a traitor. When I was in prison, I felt as though it was a microcosm of Israeli society. Everybody was together, even detainees from Kiryat Arba.[6] We'd play backgammon and laugh together. I noticed that people looked at the situation as if it were a game—like a football match with one winning side. But it's not like that. There can't be only one winning side. Either we both win, or we both lose.

I'm always moved to see Arabs and Jews together. This means that a sense of separation is still deep inside me. All I can do is keep working on myself. Treating people equally is not an innate quality. In

5. See Chapter 4, note 7.
6. A Jewish settlement on the outskirts of Hebron that is considered ideologically extreme.

nature, the strong always win. But a culture can place a priority on equality as a value. People can be convinced that it's worth recognizing one another as equals.

CHACHAM: But most of the time cultural constructs hinder our ability to see other people equally.

LOTEM: When I was a kid, we believed that Arabs were bad and leftists were weird. We used to go watch Arab laborers. We liked to see how they drink water without touching their lips to the bottle. The Arabs I knew were all simple people. They seemed so remote. And just as we used to gawk at Arabs, we would gawk at people who were supposedly leftists. We thought they were the strangest creatures.

The fear of Arabs is something that everybody who was raised here is infected with. It's a hard thing to cure. People don't trust them. They arrest them just because they're Arab. It infuriates me. But today, I try not to get angry with right-wingers who hate Arabs. I understand that their hatred stems from a sense of tribal belonging. As far as I'm concerned, Imad is from my tribe, even though he's supposed to be from another. I feel closer to my friends in Ramallah and Qalqilya than I do to the settlers of Kiryat Arba. But I also recognize that the Holocaust feeds Jewish anxiety. This fear is not out of place. Many people feel persecuted; it's a real feeling. Many leftists forget that this is the case, that you can't negate people's feelings. So the question is, How do you get people to stop feeling that way?

Yuval Lotem looks strong and healthy, but also weathered by life's hardships. While most Israelis regard refusal as an unbearable rupture in their lives, he has no sense of being torn between his conscience and his loyalties. After all, he comes from a family that sees itself as the salt of the earth. He does not feel any need to prove that he belongs.

His friendships with Palestinians are abnormal in the view of most Israelis, who see all Palestinians as terrorists who come bearing explosives. Most contacts between Jews and Palestinians are those of employer (Jew) and employee (Palestinian). Yuval relates to the Palestinians on equal terms, warmly and humanely. He sees no reason to get into the nuances of politics with them.

He has chosen the path of humanism instead of studying the political roots of the conflict. He resolves the inner contradictions pervasive in Israeli ideology, like being victorious yet feeling victimized, by dealing with his conscience rather than with his fellow citizens. He tries to find equality for all, something he looks for by examining the fears that people experience equally.

His story contains all the elements of life in this country: parents who instilled confidence in him; an extended family that is angry about his refusal; a liaison officer who cannot conceive of why he wouldn't serve in Megiddo Prison; the frightened stare of a child in Gaza; his own adolescent caricatures of Arabs and leftists; the many people he worked with as a contractor; and the story of Imad Saba, exiled from his home in Ramallah.

Though most of his films do address political issues, he does not see himself as a political creature. He views the fears that inform Israeli consciousness, and, by extension, Israeli policy, as psychological in nature. These problems are not ideological, he believes, and therefore do not need a political remedy. If he were to carry through his political thinking, he would interrelate fears from the Holocaust with the fears of a Gazan child and those of his friends' children, who tremble in bed during the Israeli air raids he hears over the phone all the way from Kfar Shmaryahu.

CHAPTER EIGHT

Staff Sergeant (Res.) Ishay Rosen-Zvi

Ishay Rosen-Zvi, a 30-year-old married father of three, grew up in Tel Aviv and now lives nearby in Givat Shmuel. Ishay is a doctoral student in intellectual history and the Talmud at the Cohn Institute for the History and Philosophy of Sciences and Ideas at Tel Aviv University. He is also a fellow at the Hartmann Institute in Jerusalem, which has become an intellectual center for the elaboration of critical political thought in Israel over the past decade, alongside the Van Leer Institute.

His deceased father, Professor Ariel Rosen-Zvi, was Dean of the Tel Aviv University Law School and a prominent representative of left-leaning religious Zionism. Active in Netivot Shalom, a leftist religious movement, Prof. Rosen-Zvi struggled against the religious establishment and addressed the injustices of the occupation before it was considered acceptable to do so.

Ishay Rosen-Zvi describes the Gaza of the early 1990s, the days of the first Intifada before the Oslo Accords were signed. He was serving as a regular conscript at the time, and the process of awakening that eventually led him to refuse had already begun. Although most of the residents of Gaza still worked in Israel, the situation of most Palestinians deteriorated with the peace process. While Palestinian rule replaced direct Israeli rule, the Israeli withdrawal from Gaza has been limited in scope. The citizens of Gaza have been denied work in Israel and are barred from the West Bank. Since the signing of the Oslo Accords, most Palestinian laborers have been replaced by foreign workers.

Ishay serves as a sergeant in the armored corps. For ten years, he served in the territories, maintaining the occupation and witnessing its effects. Even though he was not blind to what was happening around him, it took time for him to arrive at the decision to refuse his orders. A year ago, he refused to perform his reserve duty in the occupied territories, a decision that landed him in military prison for two weeks. When the refusenik officers mobilized, he joined their initiative, signed the letter, and became a prominent activist among them.

Bright-eyed and with a boyish face, Ishay Rosen-Zvi speaks with great fervor. On the one hand, his words are grounded in rational analysis; on the other hand, the torrent within him threatens to overflow. His look reminds me of Bnei Aqiva, the nationalist-religious Zionist youth movement where Rosen-Zvi was trained. The discrepancy between his appearance and his ideas makes for a thrilling contrast. Yet Rosen-Zvi prefers not to talk about himself or to touch on his identity. He is quick to focus on the reality in which he operates, and to analyze its variables.

Ishay Rosen-Zvi concerns himself with ending the occupation. At the present time, he does not focus on what lies beyond that goal or with the practical political dimensions of getting there, nor is he concerned with a post-occupation political perspective. Rosen-Zvi's deep concern for his society resonates in his anxious voice. Most of his mental and emotional energies are directed at his own people. The suffering of the Palestinians horrifies him, but they do not figure heavily in his discourse. His consciousness and moral compass point to the injustices perpetrated against them, yet his conceptual boundaries are largely determined by Jewish Israel. His refusal arises first and foremost from a sense of responsibility toward his own people.

Unlike most of the refuseniks, Ishay Rosen-Zvi hails from religious

Zionism, those who wear knitted yarmulkes. Most of those who do so are identified with the settlers. Ishay belongs to a small camp within that camp. Many of his relatives live in the settlements. His wife, a doctoral student in physics, is the niece of a member of an extreme Jewish terrorist cell in the so-called Jewish underground. Her uncle participated in a plot to bomb the mosques on the Temple Mount and abetted the murder of students at the Islamic College in Hebron. Ishay himself lived in a settlement as a yeshiva[1] student, a yeshiva known for its political moderation, but located in a settlement nonetheless. This was a contradictory place, where talk of returning the settlements took place from within the settlement. Rosen-Zvi moved away from that milieu and took a critical position toward it, a position for which his teachers, rabbis, and friends have denounced him.

———

CHACHAM: Can you describe what you witnessed in the occupied territories?

ROSEN-ZVI: In Gaza, I saw people living in shameful poverty. My heart ached for them. At the checkpoints, they look at you fearfully. They stand waiting to get through to work in Israel. Whether they pass through depends entirely on the commander's mood that day. They stare at you with humiliated, furious eyes. Some of them could be my grandparents. I don't know what I would do if I saw my father like that. Yet I faced children who saw their fathers degraded day in and day out. Gradually, I came to understand that my duty was to ensure that the Palestinians remained this way. I tried as hard as I could to be humane, but it's not a question of etiquette. Whatever you do, however you act, you have one purpose: to deny people their freedom. I felt

1. See Chapter 6, note 4.

more than discomfort, I felt schizophrenic. Going from Tel Aviv to Gaza, I felt like Dr. Jekyll and Mr. Hyde. I didn't talk about it because it was too embarrassing.

I'm ambivalent about giving examples of what happened. They're used to obliterate the norm. In other words, if you publicize a particular incident, it's presented as the exception to the rule. This is precisely what I don't want to do. I want to discuss the norm, the force that has to be exercised to deprive a people of their rights. When you engage in describing specific incidents, you arrive at what I like to call the thesis of the sadistic commander. He's the one who gets excited and moves beyond the call of duty. It's not that there aren't sadistic commanders, there certainly are, but that's not where the problem is. The problem is the good-hearted leftist commander. The one who doesn't beat people and doesn't curse, but does only what he is told. The one who is ordered, "Uproot that orchard today," and does just that. No more no less, without enthusiasm, perhaps even with sorrow. And make no mistake, there are enthusiastic commanders who, when you tell them to uproot an orchard, will tear down the next one as well. Because who knows, maybe tomorrow the High Court of Justice will issue a ruling forbidding the destruction of orchards.

But that's not the story. The story of the occupation is that of the good commander, the one who feels bad that he has to uproot the orchard but grits his teeth and proceeds because somebody has to do it. It's because of guys like this that millions of Palestinians have been living like dogs without basic rights for almost two generations.

Today, however, it is imperative that we say exactly what's going on there, and in as much detail as possible. Why? Because today the urge to deny is greater than ever. People say, "Don't tell me what's going on there. I don't want to know how many Palestinians are starving while we contend with the suicide bombings." These are not innocent sentiments. Someone wants us to think that starving Palestinians are irrelevant. Patriotic support for the occupation requires denial. Journalists like Amira Hass and Gideon Levi[2] are perceived as intolerable because politicians and mainstream reporters encourage this perception. Hass and Levi disrupt denial. In this sense, testimony, or the discourse of facts, is important. What do Israeli citizens know about what's going on in the territories? What are they willing to know? What are they allowed to know?

It's the unwillingness to see the other side that shackles our ability to comprehend terror and what motivates it. You can't wage a war on terror without knowing how it's manufactured. Understanding the terrible injustices that we inflict on the Palestinians day in and day out is not irrelevant; it's urgent, especially when security rhetoric silences any critical discussion. The rhetoric of national security subsumes everything. It justifies any action, as cruel and horrendous as it may be. The lives of Palestinians gradually cease to have meaning. At the end of the day, after all the rational security claims, you realize that what makes all these atrocities possible is that "they're just Arabs."

Not a single settler's house has been moved an inch for "security reasons." Not a single settler's tree has been uprooted. But to destroy row upon row of Palestinian homes, and thousands of dunams[3] of olive trees, entire worlds, just because they're blocking the view of some company commander—that's no problem.

Since the army reinvaded the Palestinian cities in March 2002, the Israeli media have been enlisted in the service of the state more than ever. Their objective is clear: a well-functioning propaganda machine must be in place to create consensus around an ominous, insane war. Here's where Prime Minister Ariel Sharon's genius is revealed, as well as the sinister nature of our society, journalists and intellectuals

2. Israeli reporters who write about the reality of Palestinian life in the territories for *Ha'aretz*, Israel's leading liberal daily.
3. A Hebrew term for one square kilometer.

included, who remain silent in the face of the current devastation. Our duty as refusers is to expose this manipulation.

Reentering the territories is meant to pacify the public. "We must do something"; "We'll show them who's boss"; "The big, bad IDF will put them in their place." This is the logic of vengeance. But the IDF won't be able to show them anything. It can sow destruction and loss, but that's also what it will reap. You can defeat an army, but how do you defeat a people? How do you get them to submit to occupation and oppression, to live without their rights?

When we talk about the injustices perpetrated in the territories, people ask us, "Where are you living? Every day there are suicide bombings. Who cares about the women in labor at the checkpoints?" And I say, let's talk precisely about that—about the situation that has led to the suicide bombers. They didn't come out of nowhere. They hate us, and I'm not the least bit surprised. We earned it. Recently the number of suicide bombers has risen significantly. A few years ago, less than 20 percent of Palestinians supported suicide bombings. Today, it's difficult to find anyone who will criticize them. What happened? Did the "Arab mentality" change? Did everyone suddenly fall in love with radical Islam? Netanyahu[4] and his cohorts want us to see terror as a destiny imposed on us by Islam, something preordained by supernatural religious powers. They're keeping us from understanding the social dynamic and our part in its development. When you can't understand, you also can't resist. It must be stated clearly: Israeli government policies in the occupied territories are fertilizer for suicide bombings. We produce the terror. Who in their right mind thinks that more destruction and more humiliation will curb it?

The extreme right talks of a comprehensive military solution; in other words, the only way to defeat an occupied people is to destroy them or expel them. For them, the equation is simple. As long as we are

4. Former Israeli Prime Minister Benjamin Netanyahu served in office from 1996 to 1999.

here, millions of people have to live without rights. We refuseniks warn that a violent solution is no solution. Force begets force begets force. This isn't a battle for our homes. It's a colonial war to perpetuate the occupation. As such, it is doomed. We've already seen this scenario in South Africa, Algeria, and elsewhere.

Some of us met with the first conscientious objector to oppose the South African apartheid regime. There, refusal to serve in the military was punishable by seven years in prison, as opposed to the 28-day average in Israel, and incitement was punishable by death. This man sat in jail for two years in the early 1980s, until he received amnesty and was released. He told us his story, and the similarities were striking. There too, such actions weren't tolerated by the society at large. "Not now," they were told. "The terror must be suppressed"; "If you give them a state, they'll throw you into the sea." But he and others like him didn't join the ranks of the soldiers, because they couldn't collude with apartheid. They understood that it was pointless, that it couldn't last. And, most important, they understood that it was verboten. Did the handful of whites who fought apartheid and refused to partake in it weaken or strengthen their society? I have no doubt that they saved their country. The best way to serve your society is by refusing to perpetuate its injustices.

As far as I'm concerned, the question that's more important than our national morale is: "What do the Palestinians eat, now that they've been living under siege and denied work for over a year and a half?" National morale can't be constructed around injustice. Our national morale will be strengthened only after we withdraw from the territories. This is nothing but an attempt to delegitimize our dissent, just as allegations of anti-Semitism are meant to invalidate any criticism of the government.

The one and only condition for resolving the conflict is to end the occupation. Whether the responsibility is entirely ours is irrelevant.

Are we solely responsible for the situation? No. But there's no symmetry between occupier and occupied. The onus is on the occupier to grit its teeth, advance the negotiations process, and make the biggest concession.

The focus on Arafat's responsibility for the current destruction and horror is a brilliant media spin. It magically shifts the blame from the occupation to the *rais*.[5] Israelis' power games with Arafat have erased the immense frustration and disappointment that have compelled thousands of people to commit fatal and cruel acts, by presenting these bombings as the bidding of their leaders. In order to buy this, we mustn't see the real picture. We mustn't know what's happening and how the occupation works.

How does a surgical war look from the point of view of a child in Qalqilya? After months of siege and starvation, he sees his brothers, age 14 and above, rounded up in the town square while his home is bombarded so the soldiers can invade the neighbor's house. And the Israeli press appears eager to take the bait. Special war supplements have been printed, with descriptions of fierce battles in grandiose, colorful centerfolds. Songs commemorating the fallen, commonly broadcast on suicide-bombing days, have been replaced by war tunes extolling comrades-in-arms. Ah, war! The glow returns to our faces, our posture straightens, and we hit the road with our war chants.

After I refused, my rabbis and teachers came out against me. I was told I was spilling the blood of others. I admit that hurt. But I ask all those moralists, "When was the last time you were hungry? When was the last time you roasted in the sun for hours on end at a checkpoint? When was the last time a foreign army invaded your home and locked you up, together with your children, in a single room?" Every time I'm hit with a dose of criticism, which happens quite often, I recall what I saw while serving in the occupied territories, and I put things into per-

5. President or chairman, in Arabic.

spective. I know that I can no longer stand in the way of destitute laborers. Tens of thousands of people are blockaded in their villages, unable to bring home not only butter, but bread, not to mention water, and they are neither Tanzim[6] fighters nor members of Hamas. Starving people. Not from natural causes. Because of us. Because of our brave soldiers.

During the years that I served in the territories, refusal was not an option I could consider. It was precluded by the education I received both at the yeshiva[7] and at home, a leftist education, but not a radical one. You can complain, but do what you're told and don't challenge the army. In places like Netivot Shalom,[8] it was even desirable to say how terrible the checkpoints are. And yet refusal was not considered an option. Refusal became a concrete possibility only after I enrolled at Tel Aviv University and my horizons broadened. After I was exposed to other texts, people, and communities. After departing from the totality of the religious-Zionist context. I had to go through a very long incubation process, unlike today's refusers, who serve in the territories and already know they won't return. With me, everything was steeped in a deep fog that needed time to evaporate. Today, refusal strikes me as the most Zionist and patriotic thing one can do.

Refusal is also a civic obligation. Whoever was willing to participate in apartheid or in the genocide in Kosovo betrayed his basic duty not only as a human being but also as a citizen. That's my response to the debate over the democratic legitimacy of our actions.

As for your question about our supposed absolute right to the land, I neither speak nor think in terms of absolute rights. There are memories, and historical connections, and myths. I don't diminish the potency of Jewish myths about this country. They nurture me. But someone who respects his own myths can't denigrate those of another.

6. A Palestinian militia.
7. See Chapter 6, note 4.
8. A movement "for Judaism, Zionism, and Peace."

I don't subscribe to metaphysical and metahistorical political thinking. The radical left thinks in terms of original sin when it comes to Zionism, and the messianic right thinks in terms of redemption. The game should be thinking in terms of the subtle shades, the small historical stories, specific historical constellations.

CHACHAM: The Israeli consensus is that the territory within the 1948 borders is unquestionable. Those are the borders decided upon by the international community after the '48 war. The extreme right maintains its ancestral claim to the entire land. The radical left talks about responsibility for the tragedy of the Palestinian people going back to 1948, when 700,000 Palestinians were uprooted from their land and became refugees. In what terms would you talk about a historical compromise?

ROSEN-ZVI: The place where the radical left and the radical right meet is where there's no perceived difference between the borders of the state set in 1948 and the borders of the territories occupied in 1967. No difference between Ariel, a settlement beyond the Green Line, and Kfar Saba, a town inside the Green Line, between the University of Tel Aviv, built on the ruins of the Palestinian village of Sheikh Mounis destroyed in 1948, and Kfar Darom, a settlement in the Gaza Strip. I don't buy this rhetoric. Not from the radical left, and certainly not from the extreme right.

Today, we know about the injustices committed against the Palestinian inhabitants of this land during the establishment of the state, and it's important that we remember them. But it is equally important not to place all the blame under the single heading *Zionism*. In 1948, there was a struggle for our homeland. In 1967, there was a struggle for our neighbor's homeland. That struggle intended to evict him, or at least to turn him into a tenant. This difference should not be blurred.

The law of the land, meaning Israeli law, does not apply in the territories. Today all the inhabitants of the State of Israel, Jews and Arabs, are its citizens, be they more equal or less equal. We have not fulfilled our responsibilities on this front, and this warrants further discussion. But at least all the permanent inhabitants of Israel, Jews and Arabs alike, are citizens. At least officially, there is one single rule of law in Israel. In the territories, there's no law and no citizenship, and that's why we're there on borrowed time. The occupation must end. That will be a day of celebration for Israel. It won't solve our problems, but it will signal the moment when we can begin to address them.

You ask me if I hope for coexistence with the Palestinians. Of course I do; why wouldn't I? As it says in the Talmud, "I am a creature of God, and he is a creature of God."[9] But we mustn't let this vision divert our attention from the urgent task of ending the occupation. Talking about reconciliation and utopian peace serves the rightists in their attempt to perpetuate the status quo and avoid practical compromises, under the guise of claiming that such talk does not offer a genuine peace. We must examine how this functions in the larger political framework. Several days ago, I wrote a response to just this type of hyperbole, and in it I said, "Don't talk about peace, Netanyahu talks about peace. Talk about ending the occupation."

I am a student of Professor Adi Ophir.[10] I accept his philosophical contention that fighting evil precedes envisioning the good, logically, politically, and morally. In order to identify evil and fight it, one need not paint an idyllic picture of the world, as many philosophers from Plato onward maintained. You can point and say, "This is bad,"

9. Talmud *Bavli Berachot*, p. 17a.

10. Adi Ophir, a professor of philosophy at Tel Aviv University, refused to serve in the occupied territories in 1989. Prof. Ophir and a few other professors at Tel Aviv University do not hide their attitudes on the obligation to refuse. They have enabled a situation in which refusal is an option, a model of possible conduct. And, unprecedentedly, they have preserved a political discourse in which it is legitimate to talk about refusal.

without a utopian vision as a reference point. Utopia is a scary, dangerous place. Consider Plato's republic, in which those who didn't fit the utopian mold were expelled. Consider the Third Reich, also a utopian model. I don't know how things will look in the end, and, to be honest, I don't concern myself much with that. I know what's really urgent, and I know that we must fight against what's happening right now, and that's enough for me.

The road to peace was never taken. Construction in the settlements was never halted. On the contrary, ever since Oslo, building in the settlements has boomed. The Palestinians have never had a genuine partner in peace. A government that talks peace but continues to build settlements in occupied territory is either fraudulent or stupid. While I don't rule out the possibility that the latter is true, I tend to think that the answer is the former.

When we end the occupation, evacuate the settlements, and establish a Palestinian state, the Israeli-Arabs' issues will come to the fore. Then we'll have to contend with the price of linking Judaism to our political structure. No doubt this will reveal its problematic qualities, like forbidding the sale of state lands to non-Jews or the use of ethnic criteria in place of naturalization laws. We will also have to address the reality in which Israel's non-Jewish citizens systematically encounter discrimination. It's ridiculous for us to speak of equality. This fallacy is obvious to all. Just look at the state budget and see how the Arab communities have been discriminated against in education, infrastructure, and health services.

At the same time, I can't be counted among those who are in a hurry to forgo a nation-state. Nor am I inclined to unleash my wrath at the fathers of Zionism. We must remember the conditions in which they operated. I don't intend to ignore the price, or the injustices, but

I do believe that they founded something truly remarkable here. We must dedicate our souls to preserving it.

The lessons of the twentieth century teach us that we're headed toward more nationalism. More nation-states are being built than are being dismantled. Eastern Europe is teeming with new nation-states, as is the former Soviet Union. We didn't invent nationalism and the rise of collectivist sentiments in times of political crisis. Look what's been happening in the United States since September 11, 2001. It's frightening to see how easy it is to evoke xenophobia and blind disdain for the Other. There, as well as here, you find the basest forms of racism. Over the last few weeks, as a result of watching too much CNN, the following question has begun eating away at me: How many innocent civilians did the U.S. kill in Afghanistan since September 11—fewer than the number killed in the World Trade Center tragedy, or more?

The real threat to the State of Israel today is the occupation. That's why refusal is practically the only Zionist position you can assume today. When refusal becomes a public act and doesn't remain a private one, it becomes a social and political option. For the first time in 35 years, every soldier has two choices: he can go to the territories, or he can refuse. Whoever goes today doesn't do so automatically. He makes that choice. Refusal has become a paved road.

Refusal is also like a bug in the system. The machine is set for self-destruction, and our job as refusers is to short-circuit it. The national-unity government allows no parliamentary opposition to speak of, and the army is one of the most reactionary players on the political field. The courts can't put on the brakes either. The judicial branch has never intervened effectively in the territories. There's almost no one who can stop this. The brakes have gone out, and I don't know to what extent we can halt this mad charge, but we have to try.

I've recently come to understand that the aversion to identifying with the refusers stems less from nationalist fervor than from the ethos of moderation. Moderation is the highest bourgeois value today. "Don't exaggerate"; "Don't kick up the dust"; "Don't speak in extreme terms." We have to get used to the idea that refusal is a powerful act, and there's no point in trying to obfuscate it with consensual statements. Refusal is an unambiguous act at a time of great ambiguity. It's a risk, and that's why it's both intemperate and un-bourgeois. This is the moment when you must take a position. Either you cooperate or you don't.

Yesterday someone told me, "I avoid extremes. The truth cannot be found on either side."

I said, "Think about the last stupid war, and don't go as far back as Germany: go to Kosovo, go to Vietnam. Think about what you'll tell your children when they ask you, 'Where were you during our stupid war?' You'll say, 'What do you mean, I avoided the extremes, I weighed everything very carefully, and I knew that the truth didn't belong to either side.' But people died. And what did you do in the meantime? You avoided the extremes."

The history of shooting the messenger is as long as that of war itself. We're not responsible for weakening society. We're delivering the news. We won't recite the same old story about how righteous we are. The messengers usually come from within the ranks, but as soon as they send word of what's going on, they're ostracized. That's what happened to us. People in our movement said they didn't want to be identified with the radical left. Someone told them, "You *are* the radical left. Maybe yesterday you weren't, but today you are. Even if you don't think of yourselves in those terms, someone has already put you there."

CHACHAM: As a messenger, do you want to speak as one soldier bearing witness to what you saw, or do you carry a message for the future?

ROSEN-ZVI: The key is secularization, in the sense of taking what is metaphysical out of our ancient myths. We can't do without myths, but we can treat them with irony. What does the Wailing Wall mean to me? It means all kinds of things, but I can also see it in proportion. As soon as you renounce absolutes and forgo the metaphysical, mythical world in which this land is ours because Abraham was here, you can maintain a sense of nationalism without denying the rights of the Other. These things can exist concurrently. Metaphysical rhetoric really is the most frightening of all. Once we thought it belonged to Gush Emunim[11] alone, but today it has permeated Zionist dialogues in general. Even the Labor party spews this kind of rhetoric.

Yesha'ayahu Leibowitz said that one of the principal tenets of Judaism is that the Messiah will never arrive. Since you must await him every day, it means he will never come. In my interpretation, it follows that the present is always the present, the future is always the future, and the absolute always belongs to the future. As long as the absolute belongs to the future, the present is a present with a small p, and then everything can exist here and now simultaneously. The absolute is dangerous because it juxtaposes the light against darkness. Time stops being human history and becomes divine, and that leaves no room for irony. That's why I refuse to mix theology with politics. When you think that your enemies are the enemies of God, your moral faculties disappear. The woman at the checkpoint vanishes. When you speak the language of absolutes, you stop seeing people as human beings, and that's where the roots of the current tragedy lie.

The current use of the saying, "You have chosen us from among

11. See Chapter 6, note 2.

all nations for Your service"[12] is wrong. We must address the sense of superiority that has become so prevalent among us. It's important to remember where the "You have chosen us" actually comes from. Its origins are in an entirely different place from today's nationalism. The feeling that we are superior began as the rhetoric of consolation. Look at all the major sermons in the writings of the talmudic sages, when the people of Israel were downtrodden under Roman rule and had nothing of their own. It's in this context that they speak of their own greatness. They fantasize about their imaginary might. It's a form of consolation for the weak, and as such not very dangerous. Today, of course, the situation is totally different, because the weak have become the strong, but they continue to employ the same old rhetoric and myths.

12. A phrase from the Jewish Sabbath prayer.

CHAPTER NINE

Private David Chacham-Herson

A LETTER FROM JAIL

As I sit here in Military Prison Number 4, I read the terrible reports that appear daily in the press. I get no pictures, no soundtrack. I see only barbed wire.

Still, the pain outside drifts in. Revenge repays revenge; killing repays killing. Why must we cause so much suffering? Why do we inflict so much pain on others and ourselves? What is behind our sense of pride? Why is killing held so highly in our eyes?

I am a soldier in the Israeli army, imprisoned for refusing to take part in the oppression of a people. My position arises from the feeling that you cannot be a Jew, the son of a refugee people, and oppress refugees. I am a Jew and a God-fearing man, and as such I am forbidden to deny others freedom by serving in occupied territory.

I am imprisoned, and yet I feel more freedom than most Israelis I have known. My reasons are clear: I do not bear the burden of vengeance or the perversity of its gratification. Nor do I carry the shame of denial.

I care for the livelihood of all peoples. I care for people as people. I care for those who are denied the right to live like me, with food and clothes, good health and entertainment, dreams of success and a car.

I am concerned for those other people who are humiliated every day, who are denied the right to work, who are imprisoned inside their own towns and villages. I am concerned for those others whose homes have been demolished and their orchards devastated.

I know that a terrible hatred toward me is justified. That hatred leads to horrifying and perverted acts, such as those of the young suicide bombers, but it is we who create the conditions that lead to these monstrosities.

I know that the cries of exultation over killings drown out the weeping of all the victims, Jewish and Arab, widows and orphans, and all the cripples who will suffer for the rest of their lives because of someone else's pride.

My fear is different from that of most Israelis. My fear calls for corrective action, *tikkun*, and not for more destruction.

I am imprisoned, and yet I am free; but the pain runs deep. I hope that my imprisonment, and the jailing of others like me, will lead you to contemplation, contemplation of the Palestinians, and, by way of them, contemplation of ourselves.

My imprisonment does not release me from my responsibilities. My imprisonment is the only genuine way to participate in Israeli society today. Even if I were not serving in the army, I would take on this responsibility. I am not a victim. To the contrary: it is my responsibility to refuse to take part in this oppression.

I am a soldier, and I want to serve my country. It is where I find the people I love, including those who act against my position, people from the right and the left. I only want us, the victorious and mighty, to look into the eyes of those we oppress and try to understand them. Our fears will fade only when we create equality between peoples and between individuals. We will all go on living in fear as long as we deny people their elementary rights.

The victory of might is no victory at all. Rather than justify suffering, that which we inflict and that which we bring upon ourselves, we should try to resolve it through self-correction, *tikkun atzmi*. Wielding faith in *tikkun* makes us more powerful than tanks.

My cell is a foundation for my self-correction. I hope that others will look at the reality around them and contribute to change.

David Chacham-Herson

July 2001

David Chacham-Herson, a scruffy, 19-year-old with light, curly hair, is a musician who plays the French horn and the trumpet. While studying music at the high school of the Jerusalem Music Academy, he started performing classical music and jazz with professional and semi-professional orchestras and bands. He also composes his own music.

David did not grow up in an easygoing middle-class neighborhood. His social context has always been very diverse in terms of ethnicity, culture, and nationality. This is not customary here, since Israeli society is very segregated. Children usually grow up without much contact with people of different backgrounds, and his experience is an exception to the rule in many respects.

From January to August of 2001, he served in the army as a draftee, what is known in Israel as a regular conscript. At the time of his drafting, he declared that he would serve only inside the Green Line to defend Israel within its borders and would not fight in the occupied territories. Nevertheless, after four months of training, the army posted him in the occupied territories as part of a technical team that provided services to the combat soldiers. He refused his orders and was jailed for 28 days.

David is my son. When he entered the army, I had no idea how he would react to an order to serve in the occupied territories. He made his choice and acted upon it independently. Although we are a politicized home, and many of our conversations deal with ideological issues, I never anticipated some of the answers he gave me during this interview. We had talked about politics, ideology, and the army countless times before. The interview turned out to be an opportunity to talk about the related issues of his refusal more than we ever would have during our normal family discussions. Some of the ideological questions we considered elude simple answers, such as the meaning of nationalism, how to identify with the oppressed, the opacity of fear, and where we can find hope.

After David was imprisoned for the usual 28-day period for his act of refusal, he was released from the army following a recommendation from his officers. He applied for a year of voluntary National Service, an option that until very recently had been open only to young women.

For David and the other soldiers who serve in the army and at the same time refuse to serve in the occupied territories, their refusal expresses first and foremost a desire to belong. Military service is one thing, and fighting in the territories is another. These soldiers believe that their refusal truly serves their country.

———

CHACHAM-HERSON: Because I belong to this society, because I align my conscience with the common good, I cry out to you, my family, my friends, see this, I want to show you something; pay attention! Israeli society is falling apart on every front: education, the economy, employment, the uncontrolled violence. Here life is premised on hate. When I view the disintegration all around me from the perspective of someone who wants to repair what he sees, I see that it was all built on militarism and racism.

Our current situation resembles that of apartheid South Africa. The state of Israel forced a large ethnic group to live a life that no Jews would be willing to live without screaming to the heavens to protest with all their might.

Most of my friends talk about defending ourselves so the Arabs don't throw us into the sea. I look at this reality in a different way. I say self-defense works first and foremost through morality, justice, and equality. The Jews view themselves both as archetypes of the ultimate and as perpetual victims. They see the Arabs as liars and aggressors. I look at both peoples from a different point of view: I see Arabs living under the occupation, and I understand why my friends see themselves as victims after so many suicide bombings.

According to the predominant point of view, Jewish suffering symbolizes the history of suffering, at least in modern history. But holding a monopoly on suffering dismisses the suffering of others. It dismisses the resistance of the Palestinians as illegitimate. If we don't seek a solution to everyone's suffering, we will have to bear the consequences of what this inaction breeds: cruelty and unrelenting anger.

I can't argue in favor of an occupation that denies people basic living conditions in the name of the suffering of the Jewish people through the ages. If we had one bit of sanity, we'd look at ourselves in the mirror and say, "If our people fought for our freedom at any cost to preserve our identity, why must we cloak ourselves in aggression now that we have political power?"

I see refusal to serve in the territories as my responsibility to call for equality. Equality is a choice that has not been taken. We Israelis always say that the Arabs attacked us in 1948, 1956, 1967, and so on, and so we must not live with them as equals. But no one ever asks if it really was they who attacked us. Maybe their attacks were a demand for equality. Nobody realizes that we will be remembered as Goliath and they will be remembered as David.

CHACHAM: So what do you expect, that the Israeli people will relinquish the advantage, that they'll agree to give up the stronger position?

CHACHAM-HERSON: It's the responsibility of the strong to show concern for the weak. This is a moral imperative. In other words, caring for the weak doesn't mean giving up a position of strength. Such equality and justice are the preconditions for security. I don't believe in anything that will not ensure equality.

Some people prefer to ignore such imperatives. They say, "Why concern yourself with the Palestinians? You have plenty of poor people in your own town." I say you can't make those kinds of distinctions. Gaza is impoverished because the occupation stunts its development. The resources allocated to finance the occupation come at the expense of development towns.[1] In this respect, the poverty of these development towns in Israel is related to Gaza's poverty. Because I am an occupier, Gaza's poor are the paupers in my town.

My solidarity with the Palestinian people, my identification with their struggle, can be unbearable. Figuratively speaking, I know that I wield the stick that beats them. There have been times when I wanted to be the one who got the beating instead. Then I wouldn't have to bear the guilt.

But if I wallow in guilt and fail to recognize my place in my privileged, hegemonic society, my words of conscience lose their meaning. My job is to present an alternative to force to those in power. I remember Walter Benjamin's words, that we make progress by calling forth the history of the oppressed, not by immortalizing the history of the oppressors. I hope our social reality changes to the extent that we can recognize that we are the mighty, we are the occupiers, and therefore we must do something to end the occupation.

It fatigues me to talk about this. It isn't normal that I should have to worry about these things. A French journalist once told me that our refusal should have been about the loss of our youth! Who am I to say such a thing? And to say it in the face of a Palestinian child who has not only lost his youth but never had a childhood to begin with, not to mention the dream of growing up.

When I hang out with my friends, even if we're having a great time and not talking politics, they still justify their worldviews with the tired claim, "We have no choice." It depresses me to think that this is

1. See Chapter 2, note 5.

the sum total of my life. I can't even dream of hanging out with people other than my Jewish friends, all the other people who live here.

Our war is not for our existence. Our war is ideological. It's not about survival, but rather about a myth of our absolute right to the land. The occupation is not a necessity; it's the manifestation of a false belief in our ancestral right to the land from the Jordan River to the Mediterranean Sea.

Yesha'ayahu Leibowitz called "Greater Israel" a "bad dream of people interested in a war with the Arab people to the bitter end." Leibowitz posited that the only way for Israel to continue its existence was either to return to the borders of 1967 or to subjugate "the other native nation of this land." If Israel doesn't return to its pre-1967 borders, it "will be condemned to decline from humanity via nationalism into savagery."

CHACHAM: You live in a place where you're required to define yourself in national terms day in and day out, even if you don't want to. Do you see your nationality as a central facet of your identity?

CHACHAM-HERSON: I don't deny the importance of my nationality. I see myself as a Jew. And I also take responsibility for the acts of my collective. I can fight nationalism, which has caused much ugliness, and I can embrace it and say, "I maintain our traditions. There must be a reason I was born a Jew, and that's also why I need to respect those whose nationality differs from mine." If people were really comfortable with themselves, they'd have no problem with the Other. I want to know people of all nationalities. If we were willing to learn from others, we could benefit from living in the Middle East and from Islam being all around us. But when you constantly need to defend your nationality, then it turns into justification for war.

Israeli nationality is defined vis-à-vis the enemy. Nationality arti-ficially turns Russian Jews, Ethiopian Jews, German Jews, and Middle-Eastern Jews into the shareholders of a single identity based entirely on being "non-Arab."

CHACHAM: Let's talk about fear. That's a defining aspect of our lives. Increasingly, fear is shaping our consciousness, and not only in extreme situations. Absurdly enough, such situations have become routine, as with the suicide bombings. But even in quieter times, fear shapes our consciousness. It underlies our existence. A fear of the Arab mob delineates our existential boundaries. It defines our collective against theirs. Even if that fear is imaginary, its effects are no less real.

CHACHAM-HERSON: Fear is one of our biggest obstacles. We really are afraid, and there's little we can do about it. We build our security with fences and tanks and checkpoints. These mechanisms have dis-torted us. We're so busy defending ourselves from the Palestinian enemy that we've erected a wall and imprisoned our enemy inside it. Just as in the fables, if you build a wall high enough, in the end you'll no longer see the enemy. All you'll see is your own fear. Fear leads us to blindness and hatred; we can't even see who is facing us. We have to examine the source of our fears and address them, not evade them.

Maybe I'm blind, too. Maybe I'm blind to other things. Every-body has blind spots. Today someone accused me of blindness for fail-ing to see how savage and monstrous the Palestinians are. To me, he was blind; he suppressed the truth and that's the core of his anxiety. Insight is the gift of God. Only He who sees everything is not blind. And I don't see everything.

CHACHAM: I find your relativism disconcerting. Your definitions of good and evil are too liquid. You blur the differences, precluding the possibility of taking a stand. Do you dismiss criteria that distinguish good from evil?

CHACHAM-HERSON: The most important value to me as a Jew is "Love thy neighbor as thyself." The minute you truly see a person as just who they are, you cease to be blind. I strive to open my eyes, not to close them.

CHACHAM: The question is, What do you choose to look at, and what do you choose to ignore?

CHACHAM-HERSON: The soldier who shells people from a tank is blind. It's like the firing squad shooting at a single man; no single gunman knows he has the lethal bullet. The army enables this blindness, and society does too. Society tells soldiers, "Don't look back; you had to do it. Now go to the beach, you hero." If that's not blindness, what is?

CHACHAM: Do you feel like a victim of circumstance?

CHACHAM-HERSON: I'm not a victim; I followed my conscience. True, I was punished for it, but those who are fighting this supposedly unavoidable war are also its victims. They're the ones who will have to face their children one day and tell them, "What can I say; I thought we didn't have a choice." They'll be the victims of their own guilt eating away at them.

What is tragic is that the Palestinians are victimized two times over: first by the occupation and second by the desperation this occupation has given rise to. They deal with the pain of losing children who sacrifice their lives for the struggle, but who demean the value of life by taking the lives of innocent people. Once it achieves sovereignty, Palestinian society will be left with the gaping wounds of pride and guilt, liberty and bereavement.

CHACHAM: True, Palestinian society will have a lot of baggage to sort through later. They'll have to come to terms with a sense of loss so strong, with a sense of desperation so immeasurable, that it mushroomed into a question of "How many Jews can I kill?" What kind of society will they become as a result? How do you heal such wounds? Where will they find consolation?

CHACHAM-HERSON: The phenomenon of suicide bombers is a tragedy, but we must remember that the mass killing of Palestinians started long before suicide bombings.

CHACHAM: Our corruption and aggression impact the health of our society. Similarly, the Palestinians can't possibly build a healthy society on the grounds of revenge and martyrdom. But who are we to judge? We have lived for so long in a society that reveres its dead.

CHACHAM-HERSON: Perhaps that's how pain is eased.

CHACHAM: Let's talk about your general distaste for politics in the years before your refusal. In a sense, refusal was a defining moment for you. It led you to think politically.

CHACHAM-HERSON: I am preoccupied with love, not politics. When I was faced with orders that I considered immoral, I understood then and there that there are no utopias. When I was asked to go to the occupied territories to point a weapon in a Palestinian child's face, in my Palestinian brother's face, that shattered my belief that humanity always triumphs in the face of adversity. I had to face reality. I have to act in accordance with my own convictions. In the words of Job, "Depart from evil, and do good."

CHACHAM: Enlisting in the army wasn't an obvious decision for you. I never asked you before, but what does the army mean to you?

CHACHAM-HERSON: The army defends territorial boundaries. It's like the animal kingdom. Man divides himself into groups. Each group marks out a given territory and safeguards it. That's the army's purpose, as I see it. It's neither good nor bad; it just is. But when the army becomes the dominating force in our lives, it becomes dangerous.

The Israeli army defines Israeli identity. It blurs our differences and consolidates them into a singularity, a sameness. Similarly, it erases our myriad memories and formulates a single recollection. Your entry card into Israeli society comes through the army. Russians and Ethiopians become Israelis through the army.

The army hierarchy reflects society. Most of the non-elite units are made up of Mizrahi Jews. They're the ones who have to prepare the field for the officers—you know, Israel's finest, the brave and bright. It's the enlightened Ashkenazi leftist who carries the torch of the Zionist myth. He's the one who thinks the right-wing Mizrahi fighter is a barbarian. But the truth is that the Middle-Eastern Jew must demonstrate his hatred for Arabs, otherwise he will be confused with them. Only when the Mizrahis purge their own Arabness does Israeli society award them with status. Meanwhile, the Ashkenazi Jews reap the benefits of maintaining their elite status. They construct an enlightened self-image, but their attitude toward the Arabs is no different from that of their comrades-in-arms. Until the Arab Jew is allowed to embrace his identity in its entirety, we will remain a racist society.

I served in one of the lowliest units in the army. I told my battalion commander that I would not be a combat soldier in the occupied territories, because the Palestinians have the right and the responsibility to defend themselves according to the Geneva Conventions. I said that the settlements were illegal, and that I wouldn't serve in the territories since it's forbidden to occupy a civilian population. So he said, "Fine. We won't send you to the territories, and you won't become a fighter." He sent me to a unit of "jobniks," the guys who do chores for the fighters in the territories.

CHACHAM: Let's go back to your refusal. I remember the moment that led you to refuse.

CHACHAM-HERSON: We were watching the Israeli Air Force bomb Gaza with F16 fighter jets on TV. As soon as the Al-Aqsa Intifada began, I saw Palestinians demonstrating in the streets for their basic rights. When I saw how the army crushed a civilian population, when I witnessed the unreasonable force exercised against them, my choice was made. It made me sick to see houses bombarded only to demonstrate our omnipotence. They punished everyone because of the deeds committed by a few individuals, and in those days most Palestinians still considered those few to be extremists.

CHACHAM: Did you feel that you grew during your prison time?

CHACHAM-HERSON: It was a liberating place for me. Go against your conscience, and that will imprison you. Since I didn't act against my conscience, I felt like a free man in prison. Normally I feel restless when

I'm not active, when I feel as though life is passing me by. But sitting in prison made me feel active.

I learned that freedom doesn't depend on my surroundings, family, friends, not even my music, but on me. The question I faced was "How free is my spirit?" At first it was really hard. They yell at you, you stand at attention, and you perform these ritual exercises. At first, that made me furious with the system. I'd go to sleep with a sore back from all these routines. In the end, I understood that it didn't matter how much they yelled at me: I could still be free as long as I conquered my anger. After a while, I understood it wasn't so difficult to stand at attention for hours on end. If the body surrenders, the spirit soars.

CHACHAM: You also mentioned something about prison enlarging your voice.

CHACHAM-HERSON: In prison, you represent something that's bigger than you alone; you represent an entire struggle, a whole belief system. You become a symbol of the struggle. It's a powerful experience. I also discovered that when you put yourself at the service of an ideal, your ego becomes unimportant. When your words don't rise from your own selfish desires, your voice is clear. It reaches more people.

CHACHAM: And then you wrote the letter.

CHACHAM-HERSON: I wrote incessantly in prison. I wanted to write something concrete, but I just couldn't. I kept tearing up the pages. Then one day, after returning from hard work, I got hold of the newspaper during our lunch break. I saw a huge, bloody headline. This was after several days of red headlines about suicide bombings and assassinations, and our retaliation through bombing and assassinations. I couldn't take it anymore. I screamed the letter out of me in about five minutes.

I read the letter out loud to the men with me in prison. A few guys said, "You deserve three more years in jail for saying that." But most of them respected me for taking a stand. They said, "There's a guy who follows his conscience. He acts according to his values."

CHACHAM: I have a troubling question: In what way is refusal more than cleansing one's conscience? When you refuse to fight, maybe you're actually saying, "I don't want to get my hands dirty." Do you think refusal goes further than appeasing your own conscience?

CHACHAM-HERSON: Yes. My decision to refuse isolated me from mainstream society. Today, society sees me as a traitor. Tomorrow, maybe the fighters will be seen as untouchable. I wrote my letter because I wanted to have an effect on people. I also thought about the day I would tell my children that I didn't participate in an injustice.

CHACHAM: What you're saying is that the decision forced you to see things from a political perspective from then on?

CHACHAM-HERSON: In a sense. A year ago, I was a different person. Today I'm not as joyful. Maybe I'm less optimistic. I worry about a few years from now, when we'll have to contend with the choices our society has made, when the maimed and injured will come back here in hordes, and our so-called defensive shield[2] will no longer withstand their anguish. That really scares me. Maybe if I indulged in the same defense mechanisms as my friends, I wouldn't feel so tormented.

---

2. Defensive Shield is the name of the operation Israel launched in the occupied territories in April 2002.

CHACHAM: Given the suicide bombings and the devastation of the Palestinian cities and the refugee camps, it feels as though we're living in a period of endless destruction, to the extent that it's difficult to see the future.

CHACHAM-HERSON: Yes, but the future is there. The horizon doesn't disappear. Some people see the horizon as an end in sight. I see it continually receding. The unknown always accompanies us; it doesn't go away. This makes me optimistic. Every day the sun is beautiful in a different way, even though it illuminates our horrors. As it says in Ecclesiastes, "A generation goes, and a generation comes, but the earth remains forever."[3] When I look at the horizon, I see how unattainable and how perfect it is, and it fills me with hope.

3. *Ecclesiastes* 1:4.

MAPS

These maps have been selected to illustrate the continued settlement growth in the West Bank and Gaza Strip during the period 1992–2002. This period spans from before the signing of the Oslo Accords to the outbreak of the second Intifada. They show the continued political fragmentation of these areas.

ISRAEL, PRE-'67 WAR "GREEN LINE" BORDERS

The 'Green Line Borders.' These were also the cease fire lines from 1949–1967, which were internationally agreed upon.

FIGURE I

WEST BANK SETTLEMENTS, 1992

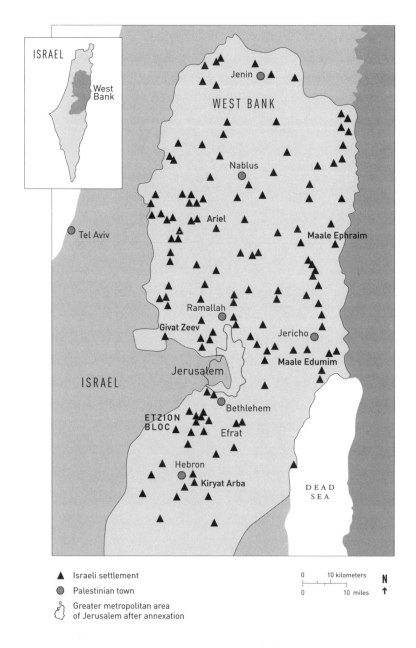

ISRAEL

West
Bank

WEST BANK

Jenin

Nablus

Ariel

Tel Aviv

Maale Ephraim

Ramallah

Givat Zeev

Jericho

Maale Edumim

Jerusalem

ISRAEL

Bethlehem

ETZION
BLOC

Efrat

Hebron

Kiryat Arba

DEAD
SEA

▲ Israeli settlement

● Palestinian town

Greater metropolitan area
of Jerusalem after annexation

0   10 kilometers   N
0   10 miles   ↑

Source: Foundation for Middle East Peace, © Jan de Jong

FIGURE 2

WEST BANK, OSLO II MAP, 1995
OUTLINING AREAS A, B, AND C

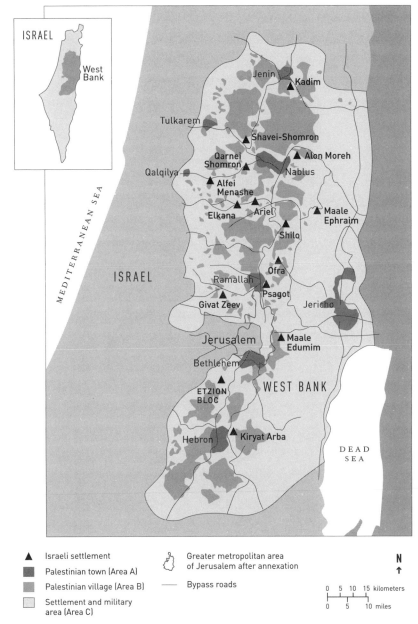

Source: Foundation for Middle East Peace, © Jan de Jong

FIGURE 3

THE WEST BANK AFTER THE SECOND ISRAELI REDEPLOYMENT (FRD)
ACCORDING TO THE SHARM EL-SHEIK MEMORANDUM, MARCH 2000

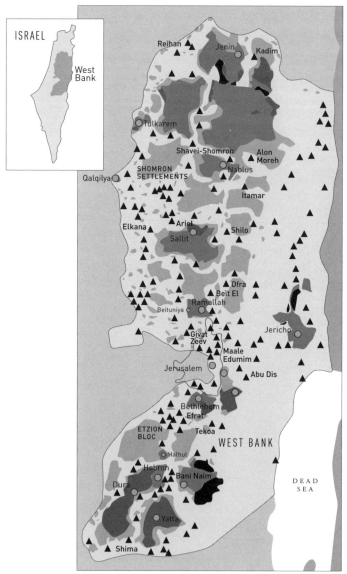

ISRAEL

West
Bank

Reihan
Jenin
Kadim

Tulkarem

Shavei-Shomron
Alon
Moreh

SHOMRON
SETTLEMENTS
Nablus

Qalqilya

Itamar

Elkana
Ariel
Shilo

Sallit

Ofra
Beit El

Ramallah
Beituniya

Jericho

Givat
Zeev

Maale
Edumim

Jerusalem
Abu Dis

Bethlehem
Efrat

ETZION
BLOC
Tekoa

WEST BANK

Halhul

Hebron
Bani Naim

Dura

DEAD
SEA

Yatta

Shima

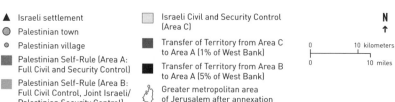

▲ Israeli settlement

◉ Palestinian town

◦ Palestinian village

Palestinian Self-Rule (Area A:
Full Civil and Security Control)

Palestinian Self-Rule (Area B:
Full Civil Control, Joint Israeli/
Palestinian Security Control)

Israeli Civil and Security Control
(Area C)

Transfer of Territory from Area C
to Area A (1% of West Bank)

Transfer of Territory from Area B
to Area A (5% of West Bank)

Greater metropolitan area
of Jerusalem after annexation

N
↑

0   10 kilometers

0   10 miles

Source: Foundation for Middle East Peace, © Jan de Jong

FIGURE 4

WEST BANK, ISRAELI SETTLEMENT OUTPOSTS, JANUARY 2002

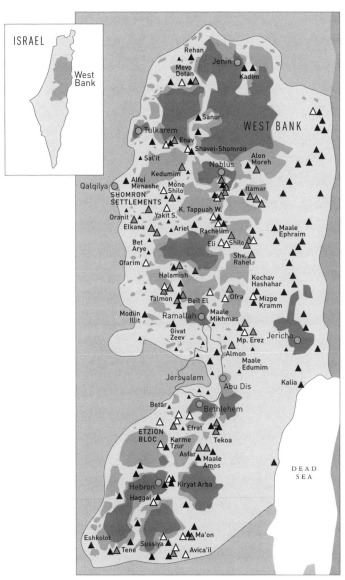

▲ Israeli settlement	■ Palestinian Self-Rule (Area A: Full Civil and Security Control)	Greater metropolitan area of Jerusalem after annexation
△ Israeli settlement outpost established from 1996–February 2001	■ Palestinian Self-Rule (Area B: Full Civil Control, Joint Israeli/ Palestinian Security Control)	
△ Israeli settlement outpost established since February 2001	☐ Israeli Civil and Security Control (Area C)	0 10 kilometers N
⦿ Palestinian town		0 10 miles ↑

Source: Foundation for Middle East Peace, © Jan de Jong

FIGURE 5

GAZA STRIP, ISRAELI SETTLEMENTS
AND PALESTINIAN REFUGEE CAMPS, 1993

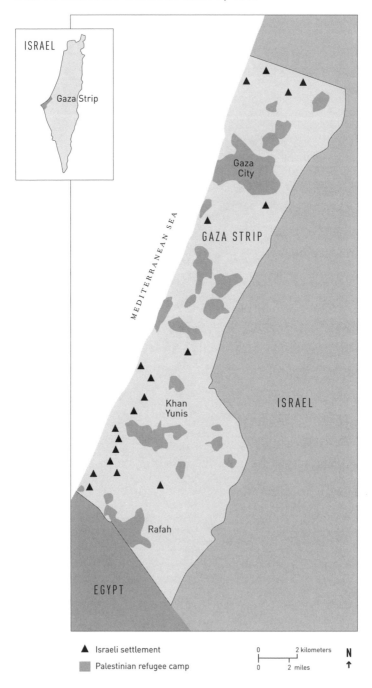

Source: Foundation for Middle East Peace, © Jan de Jong

FIGURE 6

GAZA STRIP, PALESTINIAN AUTONOMOUS AREA, 1994

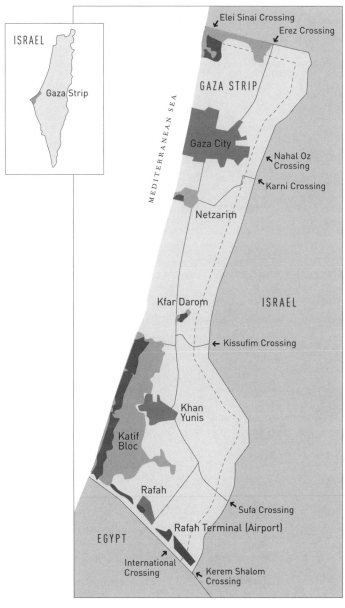

Israeli settlement area

Palestinian autonomous area

"Yellow Area" (Israel responsible for security, Palestinians responsible for civil control)

—— The Defensive Line

--- The Security Perimeter (Palestinian police responsible for security between the perimeter and the Defensive Line)

—— Bypass roads

Source: Foundation for Middle East Peace, © Jan de Jong

FIGURE 7

"BARAK'S GENEROUS OFFER," 2000

The West Bank and Gaza Strip, captured in 1967, comprise 22% of pre-1948 Palestine. When the Palestinians signed the Oslo Agreement in 1993, they agreed to accept this land for a Palestinian state and to recognize Israel within the Green Line borders. Their concession of land was a historic compromise for the Palestinians.

WEST BANK

■ Israeli
Settlement Blocs

In his offer to the Palestinians, Barak required that 69 settlements be included in these areas of the West Bank, where 85% of the settlers live. It is clear that the settlements disrupt Palestinian life in the West Bank.

■ 10% "Temporary
Israeli Control"

The concept of "Temporary Israeli Control" is unique. It refers to sovereign Palestinian land that will remain under Israeli military and civil control for an indefinite time.

■ 80% Palestinian
Control

What appears to be territorial continuity, then, is an area split apart by settlement blocs, bypass roads, and roadblocks. The Palestinian population must therefore relinquish land reserves essential for their development and absorption of refugees. They must also accept Israeli supervision of border crossings together with many other restrictions.

Source: Gush-Shalom

FIGURE 8